MENSA
LOGIC PUZZLES

Margaret C. Edmiston,
Muriel Mandell & Norman D. Willis

**OFFICIAL MENSA
PUZZLE BOOK**

Main Street
A division of Sterling Publishing Co., Inc.
New York

Library of Congress Cataloging-in-Publication Data Available

2 4 6 8 10 9 7 5 3 1

Published by Sterling Publishing Co., Inc.
387 Park Avenue South, New York, NY 10016
This book is excerpted from the following Sterling titles:
The Wizard's Book of Puzzles, by Margaret C. Edmiston & Muriel Mandell
© 2002 by Sterling Publishing Co., Inc.
The Little Giant® Encyclopedia of Logic Puzzles, by Norman D. Willis
© 2000 by Norman D. Willis

© 2004 by Sterling Publishing Co., Inc.
Distributed in Canada by Sterling Publishing
c/o Canadian Manda Group, One Atlantic Avenue, Suite 105
Toronto, Ontario, Canada M6K 3E7
Distributed in Great Britain and Europe by Chris Lloyd at Orca Book
Services, Stanley House, Fleets Lane, Poole BH15 3AJ, England
Distributed in Australia by Capricorn Link (Australia) Pty. Ltd.
P.O. Box 704, Windsor, NSW 2756, Australia

Printed in United States of America
All rights reserved

ISBN 1-4027-1637-0

CONTENTS

Before You Begin

Puzzles are a time-honored, fun-filled way of learning to reason logically—to develop thinking skills. They serve the same function for the mind as exercise does for the body. And they've been doing so for centuries.

Here are examples of many popular types of puzzles. All you need to solve most of these puzzles are paper and pencil or pen, a fresh mind, and a keen enjoyment of the challenge of a good puzzle. In a few instances, a knowledge of very simple algebra could save much trial-and-error time.

Should you get stuck, you'll find hints for some of the puzzles in the "Hints" section, where we may point out a tricky bit of language or reveal a particular approach to take. If the ins and outs of logic puzzles trip you up, read through the logic "helps" we've provided on pages 35 and 55.

Remember that, especially with logic puzzles, getting the correct answer isn't nearly as important as figuring out *how* to find it. So take your time with each puzzle and try to work it out. Use the hints, if you need them, to do it. Finally, check the explanations provided at the back of the book to see if you got it right, or where you went wrong.

WIZARD LOGIC

IN THE OGRE'S DUNGEON

The brainteasers in this section are classic problems in logic. After the first few puzzles that get you started, they all involve "if" statements. The conclusion depends on the "if" part being true.

Once you learn how to think them through, you may find these puzzles more fun than almost any other kind. Then, in "Genie Devilment," you can try dealing with several conditional statements—several "if's"—in a single puzzle, for an even greater challenge.

In the Forest

The king's only children, Abel, Benjamin and Paula, went into the forest with their friend, the elderly Sir Kay. They wanted to try their skill with their bows and arrows. Each of them started with same number of arrows. When all the arrows had been shot, it was discovered that:

1. Sir Kay brought down more game than Princess Paula.
2. Prince Benjamin captured more than Sir Kay.
3. Princess Paula's arrows went truer than Prince Abel's.

Who was the best marksman that day?

Hint on page 92.
Solution on page 107.

Captured!

Happy at the hunt, the king's children became careless and less watchful than usual. A passing ogre easily captured them and Sir Kay and took them back to his dungeon. He placed them in four cells in a row.

The cell in which Prince Abel was held prisoner was next to Prince Benjamin's. Prince Abel was not next to Princess Paula. If Princess Paula's cell was not next to Sir Kay's, whose cell was?

Hint on page 92.
Solution on page 107.

The Ogre's Boast

"I've devoured more than 100 humans," the ogre boasted.

"Surely, it must be fewer than 100," said Sir Kay.

"Well, I suppose it was at least one," said Abel.

If only one spoke the truth, how many humans did the ogre actually devour?

Hint on page 93.
Solution on page 111.

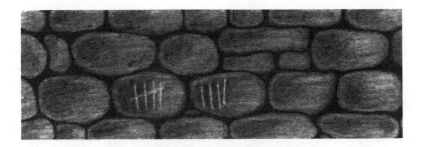

The King's Heir

The ogre's prisoners spent a sleepless night in their dungeon cells wondering what fate awaited them. The next morning, the ogre approached the king's sons. "Which one of you is the king's heir?" he demanded.

"I'm Abel, the king's eldest son," said the black-haired prince.

"I'm Benjamin, the king's second son," said the one with red hair.

If at least one of them lied, who lied?

Hint on page 92
Solution on page 107.

GENIE DEVILMENT

We never seem to get quite enough information in puzzles that pose more than one "if" statement. As in life, we're only able to come to limited conclusions—and we're likely to mess up unless we're extremely careful about organizing and recording the information we do have.

Here, the genie has presented us with classic logic puzzles more challenging and complex than those in "In the Ogre's Dungeon." I hope you are ready for them.

The First Magic Number

Here are the conditions of the first number:

A. If the first magic number was a multiple of 2, then it was a number from 50 through 59.

B. If it was not a multiple of 3, then it was a number from 60 through 69.

C. If the first magic number was not a multiple of 4, then it was a number from 70 through 79.

What was the first magic number?

Hint on page 93.
Solution on page 109.

The Second Magic Number

Here are the conditions of the second number:

A. If the second magic number was a multiple of 6, then it was a number from 40 through 49.

B. If it was not a multiple of 7, then it was a number from 60 through 69.

C. If the second magic number was not a multiple of 8, then it was a number from 80 through 89.

What was the second magic number?

Hint on page 93.
Solution on page 114.

The Third Magic Number

Here are the conditions of the third number:

A.If the third magic number was a multiple of 7, then it was a number from 30 through 39.

B. If it was not a multiple of 9, then it was a number from 40 through 49.

C.If the third magic number was not a multiple of 11, then it was a number from 60 through 69.

What was the third magic number?

Hint on page 93.

Solution on page 114.

MAGIC FORCES

Next, powerful forces and strong magic are at work. Look carefully at the changing pictures on the pages that follow. From the pattern of what has happened before, you'll be able to divine what will happen next—in other words, to predict the future!

The Missing Swords

Decorating the walls of the Wizard Zorn's secret laboratory are sets of swords, each with different magic powers. One day, to his dismay, a rival sorcerer steals in and spirits away a set of Zorn's most potent weapons.

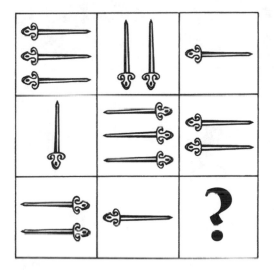

Which swords are missing?

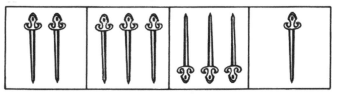

No hint.
Solution on page 111.

The Wizard Waves a Wand

When a wizard waves his wand, mysterious things happen.

Before

After

Which of the following (A through D) happens next?

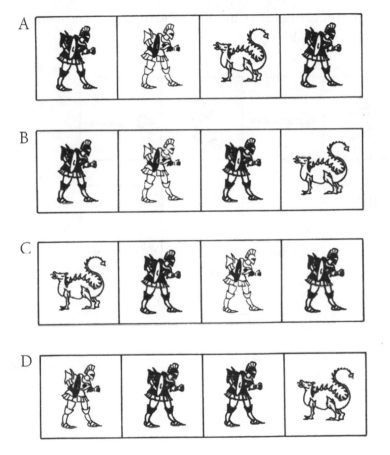

No hint.
Solution on page 116.

Knights and Their Weapons

Always preparing for combat, the knights practice with their weapons, like this:

Before

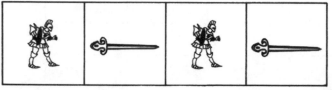

After

And like this:

Before

After

This is the way things are done now:

What happens next? Choose from A through D.

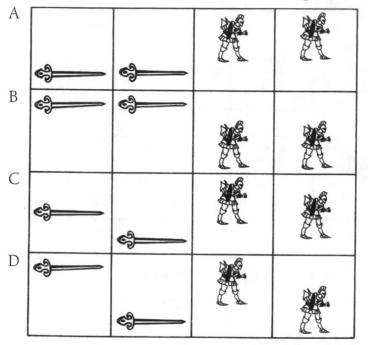

No hint.
Solution on page 154.

The Genie and the Coins

How many coins were there in the sack the genie hid?

1 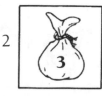 2 3

4  5

Choose one:

A   B   C   D

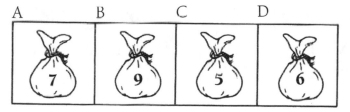

No hint.
Solution on page 128.

Genie Horseplay

What is the genie doing to the merchant's horses?

Before

After

Before

After

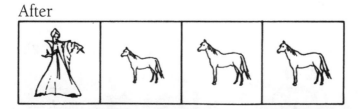

This is the way things are now:

What happens next? Choose from A through D.

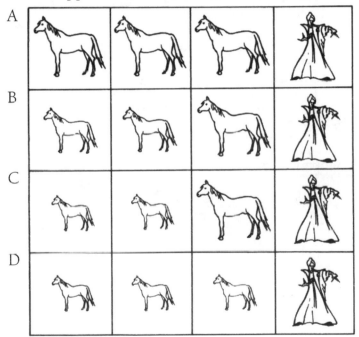

No hint.
Solution on page 136.

Genie Hijinks

To entertain himself, a genie sets things whirling.

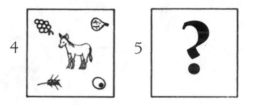

What happens next? Choose from A through D.

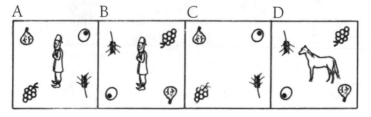

No hint.
Solution on page 157.

Medieval Merry-Go-Round

A powerful wizard has created a spectacular illusion to entertain his guests. The images he has conjured up are spinning a circle.

What happens next?

Choose one:

A   B   C   D

No hint.
Solution on page 154.

MERLIN CHALLENGES YOUNG ARTHUR

Part of the grand and mystical legend of Merlin the Magician has him serving as the wise mentor and magical helper of the young King Arthur. One can easily believe that Merlin wanted Arthur to be a wise king, as well as a brave and noble one.

To improve the young king's reasoning powers, it is likely that Merlin challenged Arthur with logic puzzles similar to those you will find in this section, involving knights, their squires, and other characters.

These traditional logic puzzles are the favorites of many people to this day.

The New Year's Eve Ball

On New Year's Eve, each of the first four knights to arrive at the castle at Camelot for the final ball of the year was mounted on a magnificent charger adorned in trappings that were the principal color of each knight's banner. In no particular order, these knights were Sir Pure, Sir Good, Sir Pious, and Sir Venerable. From the clues that follow, Arthur was to deduce the order of arrival of the four knights and the major color of each knight's trappings: blue, gold, purple, or white.

1. The four knights were Sir Pious, the knight who arrived second, the knight whose horse wore white trappings, and Sir Pure.

2. Sir Pious did not arrive first, and Sir Venerable was not the knight who arrived just before him.

3. Sir Venerable's steed didn't wear white trappings.

4. Sir Good arrived just before the knight whose horse wore blue trappings, who wasn't Sir Pious.

5. Sir Pure's charger did not wear purple trappings.

Hint on page 93.
Solution on page 114.

Who Won the Jousting Tournament?

Merlin challenged the young king with this logic puzzle as the two of them were sitting in the stands at the jousting field.

The problem was set forth as follows: at a recent jousting tournament in which a total of ten knights participated, the numbers 1 through 10 were assigned by

lot to the knights. The tournament began with a contest between #1 and #2. The winner of that contest went on to meet #3, and the winner of that second bout jousted against #4, and so forth. The last knight to remain unhorsed was the winner of the jousting tournament.

The task given to Arthur was to identify the knights in each of the nine matches, in order, and the winner of each, using the information given and the following additional clues.

1. Seven of the ten knights won no contests.

2. One contest was between #5 and #6.

3. One contest was between #7 and #9.

4. #2 did not joust against #4.

Hint on page 94.
Solution on page 117.

Name the Knights

Arthur may have been surprised when, just after he had solved the previous puzzle, Merlin asked him to deduce the names of the ten knights in the jousting contest. Merlin gave him the following clues, all of which pertain to the knights in the previous puzzle. In alphabetical order, the knights were Sirs Bad, Black, Brave, Chaste, Glory, Good, Grand, Noble, Pure, and White.

1. Sir Pure's only contest was against Sir Black.

2. Sir Brave's only contest was against Sir Noble. Sir Brave wasn't #10.

3. Sir Good's single contest was four matches before that between Sir Noble and Sir Bad.

4. Sir Bad defeated Sir Grand.

5. Sir Chaste had the position number just before Sir White.

6. No two knights whose names begin with the letter B had consecutive position numbers.

7. Sir Glory and Sir Bad had consecutive numbers, in one order or the other.

Hint on page 94.
Solution on page 112.

Merlin and the Disguises

One day Merlin, Sir Good, Sir Kay, and two squires named Alt and Maj were on a dangerous mission. It became desirable that each of the five should assume

the guises of one of the other four. As you can imagine, this was accomplished by the clever Merlin, and in such a way that no two of the five assumed the guise of the same person.

Arthur's task was to figure out who was disguised as whom. The clues that follow are sufficient.

1. Sir Good assumed the guise of the person who was disguised as Alt.

2. The person who assumed the guise of Sir Kay was portrayed by Merlin.

3. Alt assumed the guise of the person who was disguised as Merlin.

Hint on page 95.
Solution on page 116.

The Pavilions of the Champions

The magnificent pavilions of the five knights judged to be the best jousters in Camelot were set up in a perfect circle on an elevated platform north of the field where, on the morrow, they would be obliged to meet the challenges of any and all knights who dared to brave their lances. (See the diagram on page 34).

Before each pavilion, the emblem of the knight was exhibited on his shield, hung for all to see, and beside each pavilion stood the squire selected to serve the knight during the tournament. Merlin's challenge to Arthur was to determine the name of the knight at each pavilion, that knight's emblem, and the name of the squire serving him on this occasion.

The following information was given:

The Knights: Sir Brave, Sir Chaste, Sir Good, Sir Pure,
    & Sir White

The shield emblems: bear, dragon, oak tree, falcon,
    & lion

The squires: Altur, Bran, Col, Fel, & Hab

1. The pavilion of Col's knight was farther south than
   Sir Brave's.
2. Sir Brave's emblem was not the oak tree.
3. The pavilion marked "C" was the one where the
   knight's emblem was the bear.
4. Sir White's pavilion was east of only the pavilion
   where Altur was the squire and south of only the
   pavilion where the knight's emblem was the oak
   tree.
5. The pavilion of the knight served by Fel was west of
   only the pavilion where Bran was the squire, and was
   not the pavilion where the emblem was the oak tree.
6. Sir Pure's pavilion was between that of the knight
   served by Bran and that of the knight whose emblem
   was a falcon.

7. The lion was not the emblem of Fel's knight.

8. Sir Good's pavilion was further north than that of the knight whose emblem was the dragon.

9. The pavilion of the knight whose emblem was the falcon was directly across from Sir Chaste's pavilion.

Hint on page 96.
Solution on page 120.

THE LOGIC OF DISJUNCTION AND CONJUNCTION

Solving some of these puzzles, as Arthur soon learned, calls for an understanding of the logical concepts of disjunction and conjunction. For example, if I say, "I will go on vacation in June, or I will go on vacation in July," or, more simply, "I will go on vacation in June or July," you would take my statement to mean that I will go on vacation during *either* the month of June *or* the month of July, but not during *both* those months. However, should I be fortunate enough to go on vacation both in June and in July, you would still agree that my statement ("I will go on vacation in June or in July") was true. In logic, this inclusive use of "or" (disjunction) is universal. If P and Q are two statements, then: "P is true or Q is true" means that at least one, and possibly both, of P and Q are true.

We also need to agree on what is meant when we say that the statement "P is true or Q is true" is a *false* statement. Such a statement is false only when *both* statements, P and Q, are false. In the vacation example above, the statement is false *only* if I fail to go on a vacation during *either* June *or* July; otherwise, it's true.

As to the use of the word "and" (conjunction), the statement "P is true and Q is true," or more simply "P and Q are true," is a true statement *only* when *both* P and Q are true, but it is a false statement if *either* P is false or Q is false.

CHALLENGES TO THE SORCERER HIMSELF

To solve the kinds of puzzles in this section, you need to use the contradiction method. You "assume" that some fact is true, then see if the assumption leads to a contradiction (of a fact known to be true). In real life, we do this without even realizing it. If someone, for example, says, "All dogs are poodles," you know it's not true because you know of other dogs that are *not* poodles (collies, for example).

So, for these puzzles what you do is: 1) assume that a particular fact is true; 2) check the assumption against the facts you have been given, until; 3) you find a contradiction or; 4) you are satisfied there is no contradiction.

Knights, Normals, and Spies

When England was constantly under the threat of invasion, spies were sent into Arthur's land to gather secret information. Let us imagine that a spy always lied, a knight was always truthful, and all others were "normal people" who sometimes told the truth and sometimes lied.

Merlin was always on the alert to identify spies. Here are some of the situations he might have encountered.

Knights, Normals, and Spies I

Merlin encounters three individuals who are personally unknown to him. We will call them "A," "B," and "C." Merlin knows that each of the three is of a different type: one is a knight, one is a spy, and one is a normal. The three make the following statements:

A: C is not a spy.

B: A is not a knight.

C: B is a knight.

Provide a classification of each of the three people.

Hint on page 96.
Solution on page 121.

Knights, Normals, and Spies II

Merlin again encounters three individuals who are unknown to him. It is known that one is a knight, one a spy, and one a normal.

A: B is a normal and his statement is true.

B: I'm a normal.

C: B is a normal or his statement is false.

Provide a classification of each of the three people.

Hint on page 96.
Solution on page 125.

Which One Is the Knight?

Once more Merlin encounters three individuals who are unknown to him. Each makes a statement. Merlin knows only that at least one of the three is a knight. Which one is definitely a knight? Can it be determined what the others are?

A: B is a spy.

B: A is a knight.

C: Either A or B is telling the truth.

Hint on page 97.
Solution on page 108.

The Three Suspects

One of Merlin's apprentices reported an incident in which three men were tried for being spies. Said the apprentice, "The judge knew that at least one of the three was a spy and at least one of the three was a knight."

"What did the three say at their trial?" asked Merlin.

"I don't remember exactly," said the apprentice, "but I do know that, based on what was said, the judge, who is known to be a superb logician, was able to determine that only one of the three was a spy, and was able to identify him."

"What do you remember about what the suspects said?" asked Merlin impatiently.

"Well, I know that the second suspect said that what the first suspect said was false and that the third suspect said that the first suspect was a spy. I also remember that the first suspect either said he was a normal or said that he was a knight, but I can't remember which."

From this information, Merlin was able to figure out what the first suspect had said and also to determine which suspect was definitely a spy. Can you?

Hint on page 97.
Solution on page 123.

Liars and Days of the Week

In an unusual land visited by Merlin in his travels, some of the inhabitants lie on Mondays, Wednesdays, and Fridays and tell the truth on the other days of the week, while the rest lie on Tuesdays, Thursdays, and Saturdays and tell the truth on the other days of the week.

What Day of the Week Is It? 1

A Monday–Wednesday–Friday liar says, "I told the truth yesterday."

Hint on page 97.
Solution on page 118.

What Day of the Week Is It? II

In the same strange land, two citizens are encountered: one we will call "A," the other "B." A is a Monday–Wednesday–Friday liar. B is a Tuesday–Thursday–Saturday liar. On what day of the week is it possible for A and B to make the following statements:

A: Yesterday was Sunday.

B: Tomorrow is Saturday.

Hint on page 97.
Solution on page 124.

What Day of the Week Is It? III

Two inhabitants of the same land are encountered. It is known that one is a Monday–Wednesday–Friday liar and the other a Tuesday–Thursday–Saturday liar. The two inhabitants make the following statements:

A: Yesterday I told the truth.

B: Yesterday was Monday.

What day of the week is it? Which type of liar is each of the two?

Hint on page 98.
Solution on page 128.

What Day of the Week Is It?
Is It Fair or Raining?

In a still stranger land, the inhabitants are "truthers" or liars depending not only on the day of the week but also on whether the day is fair or rainy. Three dwellers are met. It is known that A lies on fair Tuesdays, Thursdays, and Saturdays, and on rainy Mondays, Wednesdays and Fridays. At all other times he tells the truth. On the other hand, both B and C lie on fair Mondays, Wednesdays, and Fridays and on rainy Tuesdays, Thursdays, and Saturdays. At all other times they tell the truth. A, B and C make the following statements:

A: It is raining and today is Tuesday.

B: It is fair or today is Tuesday.

C: It wasn't Wednesday yesterday and it won't be Wednesday tomorrow.

What day of the week is it? It is fair or is it raining?

Hint on page 98.
Solution on page 141.

The Land of Green Elves and Stolen Baked Goods

Merlin was called to the land of the green elves, where an epidemic of petty stealing was taking place. It seemed that no elf wife dared put her freshly baked goods on the window sill to cool without running the risk of some mischievous, pesky elf making off with them.

Who Pilfered the Pies?

In the first case, three elves suspected of stealing two pies were brought before Merlin. It was known that one of the three was innocent and the other two had conspired to the theft. It was also known that, of the statements made by the three, exactly one was true — not necessarily the statement made by the innocent elf.

The statements of the elves were as follows:

Arn: I am innocent.

Birn: Con is guilty.

Con: Birn is guilty.

Merlin was able to identify one of the two thieves, but of the other two, he was unable to tell who was guilty and who was innocent.

Hint on page 98.
Solution on page 125.

Who Stole the Bread?

In this case, one of the same three elves was known to have pilfered and eaten two loaves of bread all by himself. The three made statements, and it is known that the thief made a false statement. Merlin was able to use this information to identify the thief. The statement made by the three were:

Arn: I stole the bread.

Birn: Arn is not telling the truth.

Con: Birn stole the bread.

Hint on page 98.
Solution on page 114.

The Missing Meat Pastries

The same three elves were suspects in this case of the missing meat pastries. It was known that exactly one of the three was guilty and that only one of the three made a true statement; it was not known if the true statement was made by one of the two innocent elves or by the guilty elf.

The statements the three made were:

Arn: Either Birn is guilty or Con is guilty.

Birn: I am not guilty.

Con: Arn isn't guilty.

Hint on page 99.
Solution on page 130.

The Doughnut Raid

Two elves were known to have been accomplices in the daring raid on two dozen doughnuts. Four suspects were brought in: Arn, Birn, Con, and a fourth elf, Dob. In this case, the suspects' statements are not at issue. What was known was that the following were actual facts:

1. If Arn is guilty, so is Birn.

2. Either Birn or Con, or both, is innocent.

3. If Con is innocent, Dob is guilty.

4. Con and Dob don't get along, hence would not have been accomplices.

Hint on page 99.
Solution on page 131.

A Master Robbery

In this final case, the same four elves were suspects in the master robbery of two different windows on the same day. Four pies and two cakes were stolen (and presumably eaten) by the rascally thieves. The following statements were made by the four. It was known that two statements were true and two false, and that the two thieves are the ones who made the false statements. It was also known that the thieves rode horses in committing the theft. The statements made were as follows:

Arn: Con can ride.

Birn: Either Con is guilty or Dob is innocent.

Con: Dob is guilty.

Dob: Either Con is guilty or Arn is guilty.

Hint on page 99.
Solution on page 106.

MORE CHALLENGES FOR YOUNG ARTHUR

Arthur happily solved all the logic puzzles and begged for more, but Merlin waved the boy off impatiently. Then, on an afternoon not long afterwards, when the young king was bored with his regular studies and tired of practicing with sword and lance, the sorcerer decided it was time for some more tests of Arthur's

reasoning abilities. With arms uplifted and hands turned palm upwards, Merlin mumbled a strange-sounding incantation, and Arthur was enveloped in a cloud of smoke. When the smoke dissipated, Arthur found himself with Merlin in a deep wooded valley between hills.

"All of these hills contain caves," said Merlin. "Some of the caves are empty, but those that are not empty contain either a dragon or a princess. The princesses have been imprisoned by an evil witch. Any you can find will be freed."

A Princess or a Dragon? 1

"This is a puzzle I gave a Saxon spy to solve," said Merlin, "with the understanding that if he made the wrong choice, he would face the fire of a dragon, whereas the right choice would merely land him in prison."

Arthur found himself trembling as Merlin explained, "Look up the hill before you. You will see two caves. One of the caves contains a princess, and the other contains a fire-breathing dragon. Each cave has a sign above its entrance. One sign is true; the other is false.

Which cave would you choose? The Saxon spy was forced to enter the cave he chose."

When Arthur hesitated, Merlin added, "Make the wrong choice, Arthur, and I will save you nonetheless." Arthur breathed a sigh of relief and went on to make the right choice. Can you? The signs read as follows:

A.
> **At least one of these two caves contains a dragon.**

B.
> **A dragon is in the other cave.**

Hint on page 99.
Solution on page 121.

A Princess or a Dragon? II

Arthur found the preceding puzzle to be very easy, and teased Merlin, "My dear Merlin, can you not in your wisdom come up with something harder than that? Surely the Saxon prisoner is in jail and not eaten by a dragon."

"You are correct, Arthur," said Merlin, "and for that reason, I found it necessary with future spies to devise harder tasks." Merlin mumbled some strange words, waved his wand, and Arthur found himself on a hillside facing three caves labeled "A," "B," and "C." Each cave had a sign above its entrance.

"Try your hand at this puzzle," said Merlin. "The facts are these: one of these three caves contains a princess, one contains a dragon, and one is empty. Only the cave containing the princess has a true sign above it. You must figure out the contents of each cave."

Arthur found this puzzle to be much harder than he did the previous one.

Cave C is empty.	**The dragon is in this cave.**	**The middle cave is empty.**
A.	B.	C.

Hint on page 99.
Solution on page 156.

A Princess or a Dragon? III

Merlin mumbled an incantation, waved his wand, and Arthur and he ended up facing two caves on yet another hill. "This puzzle is somewhat different," said Merlin to Arthur. "There are two caves, each with a sign above it. The signs are either both true or both false. You are to determine what each cave contains. Each contains either a princess or a dragon."

The signs read as follows:

A.
> **Either this cave contains a dragon, or the other cave contains a princess.**

B.
> **The other cave contains a princess.**

Hint on page 99.
Solution on page 132.

A Princess or a Dragon? IV

Merlin whisked Arthur off by magic to a hill with four caves labeled "A," "B," "C," and "D." "In this last princess or dragon puzzle," said Merlin, "two of the four caves have signs with true statements and the other two have signs with false statements. Both caves with true statements contain a princess, and each of the two with false statements contains a dragon, so that, of course, the two caves with princesses have signs with true statements, and the two caves with dragons have signs with false statements."

The signs on the caves read as follows:

A.
The cave next to this one contains a dragon.

B.
The cave labeled "C" does not contain a dragon.

C.
One of the caves next to this one contains a dragon.

D.
The cave next to this one contains a dragon.

Hint on page 100.
Solution on page 119.

The Land of Pink and Green Fairies

Having successfully solved all the "princess or dragon" puzzles, Arthur was magically transported to the land of pink and green fairies, all of whom are female. Merlin explained to Arthur, "Real pink fairies always tell the truth, and real green fairies always lie. However, it is within my power to change a pink fairy to a green fairy, or a green fairy to a pink fairy, or both. A pink fairy disguised as a green fairy still always tells the truth, while a green fairy disguised as a pink fairy still always lies."

Can a Fairy Say "I'm a Green Fairy"?

Arthur's first puzzle was to answer the question: Is it possible in this land of pink and green fairies for any fairy to say "I'm really a green fairy"?

Hint on page 100.
Solution on page 118.

Pink or Green Fairy?

Arthur was introduced to two pink-looking fairies, "A" and "B," who made the following statements:

A: B is a green fairy.

B: I'm the same kind of fairy as A.

Arthur was to provide a classification of each fairy.

Hint on page 100.
Solution on page 133.

THE LOGIC OF "IF-THEN" STATEMENTS

Before trying to solve some of these puzzles, we need to know what it means when we say that an "if-then" statement is true or that such a statement is false.

Suppose I say, "If I stay home tonight, I will watch TV." The "if" part of this statement is the first part "I stay home," and the "then" part is "I will watch TV." Now everyone will agree that, if I stay home and I have made a true statement, I must watch TV. Also, everyone will agree that if I stay home and *don't* watch TV, I have made a false statement. But what if I don't stay home?

Suppose I visit a friend and we talk. Was my statement "If I stay home, I will watch TV" true or false? Logically speaking, the statement is considered true. But, suppose I visit a friend and we watch TV together, what then can we say about the truth or falsity of "If I stay home, I will watch TV"? Again, logically, the statement is true.

So, in formal logic, whenever an "if" statement is false, the "if-then" statement is true, whether or not the "then" statement is true. (The statement, "If horses have two legs, then I'm a monkey's uncle," is said to be a true statement. Think: if horses had two legs, *maybe I would be a monkey's uncle*.) But if the "if" statement is true, the "if-then" statement is true only if the "then" statement is true.

Three Pink or Green Fairies

Arthur soon realized that the color in which a fairy appears was irrelevant to her true nature. He told this to Merlin with some relish, but the old sorcerer merely replied, "A fairy's appearance is relevant in this next puzzle. Here there are three fairies. Each will make a statement. Provide a classification of each fairy and answer the question, 'Does A appear to be green fairy or a pink fairy?'"

A: B is a pink fairy.

B: If A is a pink fairy, then C is a green fairy.

C: B is a green fairy or A is what she appears to be.

Hint on page 100.
Solution on page 122.

The Land of Yellow and Blue Fairies

In another fairyland, the fairies, again all female, are all either yellow or blue. However, Merlin has changed the fairies' appearances so that all are striped yellow and blue. Each fairy also carries a baton which is either a magic wand or an ordinary stick. Whether magic wand or stick, all the batons look the same. Any fairy who is carrying a magic wand always tells the truth, regardless of her true color (blue or yellow), but any fairy carrying an ordinary stick always lies, regardless of her true color.

Merlin, of course, explained all this to Arthur before he transported the young king to this strange land. Then he gave Arthur some more puzzles to solve.

Yellow or Blue? I

A yellow-and-blue-striped fairy made this statement: "Either I am a blue fairy and I have a magic wand, or I am a yellow fairy, and I have an ordinary stick." Arthur was to determine what kind of fairy she is.

Hint on page 100.
Solution on page 130.

Yellow or Blue, Magic Wand or Not? I

A yellow-and-blue-striped fairy said, "I am a blue fairy and I am carrying an ordinary stick."

Arthur was asked to decide what kind of fairy she

was and to determine whether she was carrying a magic wand or an ordinary stick.

Hint on page 101.
Solution on page 127.

Yellow or Blue? II

Yet another yellow-and-blue-striped fairy stated, "If I have a magic wand, I am a yellow fairy."

Arthur was to determine what kind of fairy she was.

Hint on page 101.
Solution on page 136.

Yellow or Blue, Magic Wand or Not? II

Two yellow-and-blue-striped fairies spoke to Arthur. Merlin explained that one was really a yellow fairy, and the other a blue fairy. The fairies made the following statements:

A: I am a blue fairy and I am carrying a magic wand.

B: I am a yellow fairy and I am carrying an ordinary stick.

It was Arthur's task to figure out what kind of fairy each was, and what kind of baton each carried. Can you?

Hint on page 101.
Solution on page 140.

CHALLENGES TO A WIZARD APPRENTICE

Merlin decided to challenge a prospective apprentice with a number of puzzles, including many having to do with the science of mathematics. (You may be happy to know that many of them can be handily solved without using algebra.)

Boots for the Ogres

In a hole in the ogre's lair are three black boots, three brown boots, and three white boots. If the ogre takes out one boot at a time without looking at its color, how many must he remove in order to be certain of having pairs of boots in the same color for himself and his two ogre-ous sons? (Ogres have two left feet, hence do not need boots for the right foot that are different from boots for the left foot.)

Hint on page 101.
Solution on page 132.

Monster Heads/Monster Feet

In a land inhabited by monsters, some monsters have two heads each and three feet each, while the remaining

monsters have three heads each and four feet each. In all there are 120 heads and 170 feet. How many of each type of monster are there?

Hint on page 102.
Solution on page 126.

King Arthur Meets with King Balfour

King Arthur and four of his knights met with King Balfour and four of his knights. The ten warriors sat at a round table with Arthur and Balfour directly across from each other, and four knights between them on

each side, as shown below. In how many ways could the seats have been occupied by the eight knights if none of Arthur's knights sat next to another of Arthur's knights or to Arthur himself?

Hint on page 102.
Solution on page 157.

Tending Horses

Squires Col and Aken are each in charge of a string of horses. Col takes care of twice as many mares as Aken. Aken takes care of four times as many stallions as mares, and two more than Col takes care of, which is two more than the number of mares he, Col, takes care of. How many mares and how many stallions does each take care of?

Hint on page 102.
Solution on page 138.

How Long Did Dob Walk?

Dob, a stonecutter, comes home from work each day by ferry. His wife, Alicia, leaves their cottage at the same time each day to make the trip by mule cart to the ferry dock, meeting Dob at the same time each day.

One day Dob finished work before the usual time and took an earlier ferry, arriving at the dock one hour earlier than usual. Not wanting to stand about idly for an hour, he immediately began walking towards his cottage. Not knowing that Dob had arrived early at the dock, Alicia set out at her usual time and drove at the usual speed. On the way to the ferry dock, she met Dob and picked him up. They arrived at their cottage ten minutes earlier than usual. How long did Dob walk (assuming a constant rate of speed for Alicia)?

Hint on page 102.
Solution on page 134.

Magical Substance

Merlin showed his apprentice a bowl full of some gray-looking matter. "This is magical matter," said Merlin. "If I put a 'dash' of it into an empty bowl, it will double its amount each day and completely fill the bowl in four days." How full is the bowl (what fraction of it is full) at the end of the first day?

Hint on page 103.
Solution on page 145.

Crossing the River

Sir Good and Sir Pure need to cross a river with an ogre, a goose, and a bag of corn. Available is a rowboat which will hold two people, or one person plus either the ogre, the goose, or the bag of corn. The problem lies in the fact that a knight must always be present to keep the goose from eating the corn; a knight must always be present to keep the ogre from eating the goose; Sir Good is afraid of the ogre and won't be in that monster's presence unless Sir Pure is also present. Only the knights can row. How can everyone and everything get across the river?

Hint on page 103.
Solution on page 136.

THE LAND OF PYMM

Welcome to Pymm, a land inhabited by humans, elves, dwarves, and even Minotaurs. Here, kings rule, the Knights of the Golden Sword are the bravest heroes of the land, and armies small and large fight off invaders. In Pymm, dragons and other strange creatures (such as repulsive, monstrous glubs) are everyday menaces, wizards wield powers of good or evil, and the common folk (stoneworkers, millers, cart drivers, shopkeepers, and ferry operators) go about their lives finding amusement at fairs and joining in festivities presented at the castles of their local kings.

How Much Did Alaranthus Weigh?

Pymm has many dragons. A few years ago, one of these dragons, Alaranthus, though not fully grown, weighed 1000 pounds plus two-thirds of his own weight. How much did Alaranthus weigh?

No hint.

Solution on page 142.

Weighing a Pound of Flour

"I want exactly one pound of flour," said the customer to the miller.

"Sorry," said the miller. "My scales are faulty. One arm is longer than the other."

"Do you have some lead pellets and a one-pound weight?" asked the customer.

The miller provided these things and the customer was able to weigh a pound of flour.

How did she do it?

No hint.
Solution on page 132.

Rings for the Princesses

There were a number of kings in Pymm, each with his own base of power and his own castle. One of these, King Firnal, had a box containing three gold rings. He wanted to divide the rings among his three daughters so that each received a ring, but one ring remained in the box. How could he do this?

No hint.
Solution on page 150.

Two Riders

A knight on horseback left Belft to ride to Dalch at the same time another knight left Dalch on horseback to ride to Belft along the same road. The first knight traveled 30 miles per hour and the second traveled 28 miles per hour. How far apart were the two riders one hour before they met?

No hint.
Solution on page 153.

A Lame Horse

A knight had ridden one-third the total distance of his trip when his horse became lame. He completed the journey on foot, having spent twenty times as long walking as he had spent riding. How many times faster was his riding speed than his walking speed?

No hint.
Solution on page 124.

Jousting Tournament Number

Each of eleven competitors in a jousting tournament was given a number between 1 and 11. Sir Bale's son asked his father, "Father, what is your number in the tournament?"

Sir Bale replied, "If the number of numbers less than mine is multiplied by the number of numbers greater than mine, the answer is the same as it would be if my number were two more than it is."

What was Sir Bale's number?

No hint.
Solution on page 153.

Inspecting the Troops

An officer on horseback rides slowly down a line of sixty mounted troops placed 10 feet apart. Beginning with the first man, the officer takes 29 seconds to reach the thirtieth man. At that rate, how long will it take him to reach the sixtieth (last) man?

No hint.
Solution on page 151.

The Human Population of South Pymm

One-third, one-fourth, one-fifth, and one-seventh of the human population of North Pymm, which has fewer than five hundred human inhabitants, are all whole numbers, and their sum is exactly the human population of South Pymm. What is the human population of South Pymm?

No hint.
Solution on page 149.

Measuring Two Gallons of Cider

"I want 2 gallons of cider for me and my pals," said Mongo to the shop owner.

The shop owner, who sold cider only from a huge barrel, replied, "I have a 3-gallon container and a 4-gallon container. Will you use one of those and guess at the amount?"

"I don't need to guess," said Mongo. "I can measure exactly 2 gallons using the containers you have."

How can Mongo do this?

No hint.
Solution on page 149.

WIZARDS, DRAGONS & OTHER MONSTERS

Chased by a Glub

Pymm is inhabited by an unknown number of hideous monsters known throughout the land as glubs. Glubs live underground, but can rapidly burrow to the surface if they smell a human—one of their favorite treats.

Phipos was only 5 feet away from a glub when he saw the fat, swollen monster advancing toward him. Phipos knew that he and the glub ran at the same rate and walked at the same rate (which was, of course, slower than their running rate), but Phipos also knew that the glub could spray him with an irritating fluid from almost 5 feet away. So he immediately began to run toward the safety of a fort several miles in the distance. At the same instant, the glub started chasing after Phipos.

Curiously, Phipos reached safety by first running half the time it took him to cover the distance to the fort, then walking half the time. The glub, which ran the first half of the distance to the fort and walked the other half, was never closer to Phipos than the original 5 feet. Can you explain this?

No hint.

Solution on page 128.

How Far Apart Were the Dragons?

The dragons Argothel and Bargothel enjoy getting together for fiery conversations. They live some distance apart, each in his own cave. One day Argothel left home to visit Bargothel at exactly the same time that

Bargothel left home to visit Argothel. The day being most agreeable, both dragons decided to proceed at a rather leisurely rate, for dragons. So, rather than flying, they walked. Argothel walked at a constant rate of 24 miles per hour and Bargothel at a constant rate of 36 miles per hour.

How far apart were they 5 minutes before they met?

No hint.

Solution on page 143.

The Farmer and the Hobgoblin

A farmer was at work clearing a rocky field for planting when a hobgoblin approached him. The hobgoblin promised the farmer great wealth if he followed these instructions:

"Pick up a stone and carry it to the other side of the field. Leave the stone there and pick up another stone and drop it on this side of the field. Continue doing this, and each time you cross the field and return, I will double the number of coins you have. However, because I don't want you to be overly rich, you must pay me sixteen coins each time after I have doubled your money."

The farmer, thinking only of the doubling of his
money, readily accepted. Even after giving sixteen
coins to the hobgoblin following his first crossing, he
did not take the time to figure out what would happen
if he continued with the hobgoblin's bidding.

After four crossings, the farmer was not only too
tired to move, but he also had to give the hobgoblin
his last sixteen coins. The farmer's pockets were empty
and the hobgoblin went away laughing.

How much money did the farmer start with?

Hint on page 103.
Solution on page 139.

Wizard Rankings

Every Saturday at Pymm's End, a peninsula at the tip of southwest Pymm, there is a ranking of Pymm's End's six resident wizards. The rankings are based on the wizards' feats of magic for the previous six days. The highest ranking is 1 and the lowest is 6.

The rankings published on the Saturday before last listed Alchemerion highest because a spell he cast had imprisoned an evil dragon inside an iceberg. Others listed were: 2. Bogara, 3. Chameleoner, 4. Deviner,

5. Elvira, and 6. Fortuna.

In last Saturday's rankings, each wizard was ranked in a different position from that of the previous week. The following facts are known:

1. Bogara's change in ranking was the greatest of the six.

2. The product of Deviner's rankings for the two weeks was the same as the product of Fortuna's ranking for the two weeks.

What were the new rankings?

Hint on page 103.
Solution on page 142.

Did the Dragon Catch Pryor?

The dragon Wivere smelled half-elf Pryor at the same time that Pryor, who had been hunting in the forest, noticed smoke and fire rising from the direction of the dragon's mountain cave. Pryor then realized the dragon was active and might try to catch him. Knowing that Wivere was afraid of water, he began to run toward the seashore. Wivere smelled Pryor but hesitated for 6 seconds before he began to run after the half-elf. The dragon ran because his wings were underdeveloped, compared to his ancestors' larger ones.

Wivere was 5 miles directly north of Pryor when Pryor began to run toward the sea 2 miles directly to his south. Pryor, who could run much faster than a human, ran at a rate of 20 miles per hour over the 2-mile distance.

Wivere's speed, however, was not constant. He ran the first mile at a rate of 20 mph, the second mile at a rate of 40 mph, the third at a rate of 80 mph, the fourth at a rate of 160 mph, and so forth—doubling his speed after running each mile. Did Pryor make it to the safety of the sea?

No hint.
Solution on page 158.

Minotaur Fighters

Three Minotaur leaders lent each other fighters from their armies. First, Logi lent Magnus and Nepo as many fighters as each already had. Later, Magnus lent Logi and Nepo as many fighters as each already had. Still later, Nepo lent Logi and Magnus as many fighters as each already had. Each leader then had forty-eight fighters. How many fighters did each have originally?

Hint on page 104.
Solution on page 156.

Human vs. Minotaur

A human warrior must fight seven competitors with his lance. Six of the seven are humans, and one is a huge Minotaur with a fierce reputation. The warrior is certain he will lose the battle with the Minotaur. He is about to end his life quickly by surrendering to the Minotaur's lance, when the Minotaur decides to issue a challenge.

"Arrange us seven competitors in a circle," he says. "Choose a competitor from this circle and, moving clockwise and counting that competitor as the first position, count to the seventh warrior and fight him. From there, assuming you win the contest, count seven more places clockwise. Continue in this way until you reach my place on the circle. If you manage to defeat all the others before your turn comes to fight me, I will spare your life."

How can the human warrior make sure the fierce Minotaur is his seventh competitor?

No hint.
Solution on page 152.

EVERYDAY LIFE IN PYMM

At times when they were not being interfered with by the doings of wizards and sundry monsters, the people of Pymm went on with their daily routines—eating, building, traveling here and there. In doing so, they often found themselves faced with puzzles to figure out. Here are some of them. Isn't it strange that so much of daily life concerns mathematics?

How Many Cakes?

A banquet was given to celebrate a truce in East Pymm that put an end to clashes between humans and elves. Citizens from all races of East Pymm—humans, elves, dwarves, and half-elves—came together at the banquet.

After a huge dinner, sweet cakes were served for dessert. The first four beings at the banquet table emptied the first plate of cakes. (Luckily the castle cook had made enough sweet cakes for everyone to eat.) Heartnik, a human, took one-fourth of the cakes on the plate. Scowler, a dwarf, took one-third of the remaining cakes. Then Goodin, an elf, helped himself to half of the cakes left. Finally, Loglob, a half-elf, ate six cakes—all that were left on the plate.

How many cakes were on the plate in the beginning, and how many did each being take?

No hint.

Solution on page 135.

To the King's Castle

All the villagers in the realm of King Arthur were invited to a Christmas gala held at the king's castle. Alf and his wife, Beryl, left their cottage at 11 A.M. that morning and traveled by ox cart to the castle. At 11:30, an eager and impatient Beryl asked Alf, who was driving at a fast pace, "How far have we gone, dear?"

Alf replied, "Three times as far as the distance from here to the inn, where we will stop and have some nourishment."

The couple stopped at the inn for food and departed at 1:00 P.M. to continue their journey. Having over-eaten, Alf became sleepy and drove much slower than before their stop at the inn. Afraid of being late, Beryl asked her husband, at 2:00 P.M., exactly 2 miles from the point where she had asked her first question, "Do we have much farther to go, Alf?"

Alf mumbled, "Three times as far as we have come since leaving the inn." Beryl then demanded that she take over the driving, to which a sleepy Alf readily agreed. The couple finally arrived at the castle at 3:30 in the afternoon. Despite the long journey, both thoroughly enjoyed all the festivities. What was the distance from the couple's cottage to the castle?

Hint on page 104.
Solution on page 154.

Building a Bridge

The dwarves Dobbit and Mobbit are building a bridge over a narrow stream. Dobbit can do the job alone in 30 hours; Mobbit can do the job alone in 45 hours. Dobbit worked on the project alone for 5 hours before Mobbit joined him. The two then finished the job together.

How long did it take the two to finish the job that Dobbit had started alone?

Hint on page 104.
Solution on page 137.

What Time Does the Wagon Driver Leave His Hut?

Once a week a wagon driver leaves his hut and drives his oxen to the river dock to pick up supplies for his town. At 4:05 P.M., one-fifth of the way to the dock, he passes the smithy. At 4:15 P.M., one-third of the way, he passes the miller's hut. At what time does he leave his home? At what time does he reach the dock?

Hint on page 104.
Solution on page 145.

Meeting the Stone Cutter

Every morning, a cart driver leaves the stone quarry to drive to the ferry landing, where he picks up an arriving stone cutter. The driver arrives at the landing at 6:00 A.M. and takes the stone cutter back to the quarry.

One morning, the stone cutter woke up before his usual time, took an early ferry, and, once across the river, began walking to the quarry. The cart driver left the quarry at his usual time and met the stone cutter along the road to the ferry landing. He picked up the stone cutter and took him the rest of the way to the quarry. The stone cutter arrived 20 minutes earlier than usual. At what time did the cart driver meet the stone cutter?

Hint on page 104.
Solution on page 147.

How Early Was the Barge?

Every day a cart was sent from a village to meet a barge at the river dock. One day the barge arrived early, and the cargo normally picked up by the cart was immediately sent toward the village by horse. The cart driver left the village at the usual time and met the rider along the way, after the rider had traveled for 8 minutes. The rider handed the load to the cart driver, who went back to his village, arriving home 24 minutes earlier than usual.

How many minutes early was the barge?

No hint.
Solution on page 148.

How Many Handshakes?

Fifteen knights were invited to a sumptuous meal at the castle in Belmar. Before sitting down, each of the fifteen knights shook hands with each of the other knights.

How many handshakes occurred?

No hint.
Solution on page 155.

How Many Schlockels?

Altus says to Bott, "Can you figure out how many schlockels I have in my pockets?" He then gives Bott three clues:

1. If the number of schlockels I have in my pockets is a multiple of 5, it is a number between 1 and 19.

2. If the number of schlockels I have is not a multiple of 8, it is a number between 20 and 29.

3. If the number of schlockels I have is not a multiple of 10, it is a number between 30 and 39.

How many schlockels does Altus have in his pockets?

No hint.

Solution on page 152.

A Round-Table Arrangement

The brothers Bob, Cob, Hob, Lob, Rob, and Tob always take the same seats at their round dinner table. The following diagram indicates their seating. The following is known:

1. Lob's seat is separated from Bob's seat by exactly one of the other brothers.

2. Hob's seat number differs from Cob's and Lob's, positively or negatively, by 2 and 5, in one order or the other.

3. Cob's number is 1 larger than Rob's number.

4. Bob's number is either 1 larger or 1 smaller than Tob's number.

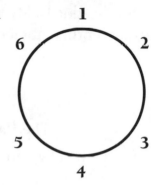

Which brother sits in which seat?

No hint.
Solution on page 144.

The Sons of Blythe

Noblewoman Blythe said to noblewoman Alexis, "I have three sons. They are all less than 10 years of age, and the product of the ages of the two youngest equals the age of the one who has the greatest age. How old are they?"

"I can't find their ages from that information," said Alexis.

Blythe added, "My final clue is that the sum of their ages is a prime number." How old are Blythe's sons?

No hint.

Solution on page 149.

The Daughters of Alexis

After she had figured out the ages of Blythe's sons, Alexis herself, who has three daughters, asked Blythe to attempt to figure out their ages. "Your first clue is that the sum of their ages is 11," said Alexis.

"That is not enough information," replied Blythe.

"The product of their ages is either 16 years less or 16 years more than your age," added Alexis.

"Still not enough," said Blythe after careful thought.

"The daughter whose age is the greatest is learning to play chess," said Alexis.

Blythe was then immediately able to determine the ages of Alexis's three daughters. What were their ages?

Hint on page 105.

Solution on page 150.

How Far From Castleton to Devil's Peak?

A horseman left Castleton and rode toward Devil's Peak at the same time that a second horseman left Devil's Peak and rode toward Castleton using the same route. The two met for the first time at the point on the route that is four miles from Castleton.

The two horsemen continued riding on to their destinations, then turned and rode back toward home at the same rate. Again they met, this time two miles from Devil's Peak.

Assuming both riders traveled at a constant speed, what is the distance between Castleton and Devil's Peak and what was the relative speed of the two riders?

Hint on page 105.

Solution on page 145.

How Did the Archers Cross the River?

A company of archers had to cross a river that had no bridge across it and was too deep to ford. They had just about given up on finding a way to do this when one of them saw two children on the river in a small rowboat. The boat was large enough to hold the two children or one archer, but was too small to hold two archers, or even one child and one archer. How did the archers get across the river?

No hint.
Solution on page 148.

How Can Everyone Cross the River?

A half-elf, an elf, a human, and a dwarf have to cross a river from the town of Ak to the town of Tok. They have a boat that will hold any two of the four, but no more.

Long-standing animosities exist between certain of these four beings, which make it undesirable for certain ones of the four to be together as pairs. While the half-elf gets along with the other three beings, the elf dislikes the human. The human dislikes the dwarf. The elf and the dwarf like and respect each other. How can the four beings cross the river if only the half-elf does the rowing, and no uncongenial pairs are together alone?

No hint.
Solution on page 137.

Feeding the Horses

Distal had enough hay and corn to feed his six horses for only 30 more days of the harsh winter, not for the remaining 75 days before spring arrived. On the seventh day, before feeding time, Distal sold four of his horses. Will he be able to feed his remaining two horses for the rest of the winter?

No hint.
Solution on page 127.

HINTS

In the Forest

Take one statement at a time and make the comparisons.

Captured!

Draw the cells and the people in them so no statement is contradictory.

The King's Heir

Consider the possible true-false combinations:

	1	2	3	4
Black Hair	T	T	F	F
Red Hair	T	F	T	F

The Ogre's Boast

Which statements are not possible? Which statements contradict one another? Use the following "truth table" to organize the possibilities:

	A	**B**	**C**	**D**	**E**	**F**	**G**	**H**
Ogre	T	T	T	T	F	F	F	F
Kay	T	T	F	F	T	T	F	F
Abel	T	F	F	T	T	F	T	F

Magic Numbers (First, Second & Third)

For each of the magic numbers, make a chart involving all the possible numbers, such as the following:

50	51	52	53	54	55	56	57	58	59
60	61	62	63	64	65	66	67	68	69
70	71	72	73	74	75	76	77	78	79

Cross out those numbers that contradict any of the statements.

The New Year's Eve Ball

Make up a chart, using rows and columns, and enter into it the facts from clue 1 to obtain the following, in which one line is used for each knight.

	Knights	**Order of Arrival**	**Color**
1.	Pious		
2.		2nd	
3.			white
4.	Pure		

Use the other clues to finish filling in the chart.

Who Won the Jousting Tournament?

Keep in mind that every time there was a contest there was a winner and a loser. Try to determine which knights definitely won no contests and which did win one or more contests. Clues 2, 3, and 4 will determine the numbers of the three knights who, by clue 1, won one or more contests. Then use the rules by which the tournament was conducted to determine the opponents in each contest and the results of their meeting. (Special hint: from clue 3, #8 must not have won any bouts.)

Name the Knights

Make a list of the numbers of the knights—#1 through #10, leaving a line for each number—and fill in the names as you determine them. Certain clues will tell you the names of the three knights who won a contest—actually we know one of them won two contests, a second won three, and the third won four. So you can begin by writing their names down on lines 1, 5, and 7. When you determine which one of the three names belongs on each line, cross out the other two names. (Special hint: clue 3 is a key clue.)

Merlin and the Disguises

Make a chart and put in it the information from clues 1 and 3 as follows:

	Person's Name	**Person's Disguise**
1.	Sir Good	Person who was disguised as Alt
2.	Person who was disguised as Alt	Alt
3.	Alt	Person who was disguised as Merlin
4.	Person who was disguised as Merlin	Merlin
5.		

First, determine who was disguised as Merlin. By clue 3 that person wasn't Alt. Assume it was Sir Good. Do you find a contradiction? Assume it was Sir Kay. Do you find a contradiction?

The Pavilions of the Champions

Make up a chart as follows:

	Knight's Name	Emblem	Squire's Name
A			
B			
C			
D			
E			

Begin with clue 3, and then use clue 4. Fill in the chart as you solve the puzzle.

Knights, Normals, and Spies I & II

The way to do these puzzles is to make a chart of all the possible combinations. Then, for each combination, look for any contradiction. If the puzzle has a valid solution, only one combination will satisfy all the given facts. The possible combinations are shown in the following chart:

Knight	A	A	B	B	C	C
Spy	B	C	A	C	A	B
Normal	C	B	C	A	B	A

Which One Is the Knight?

Start with C's statement.

The Three Suspects

Consider the four possibilities for A.

A said he was a knight and he was a knight

A said he was a knight and he was not a knight

A said he was a normal and he was a normal

A said he was a normal and he was not a normal

Which one of the above satisfies the given facts?

What Day of the Week Is It? I

Make a list of the days of the week. Write down beside each day whether the person lies or tells the truth on that day Now, on which day could he have said, "I told the truth yesterday"?

What Day of the Week Is It? II

First, decide whether (a) both statements are true; (b) both statements are false; or (c) one statement is true and one is false. Now ascertain the one day of the week that satisfies your conclusion.

What Day of the Week Is It? III

First, decide on what day or days A could have made his statement if (a) he were a Monday–Wednesday–Friday liar and (b) he were a Tuesday–Thursday–Saturday liar. Then do the same for B. Figure out on what day both statements could have been made.

What Day of the Week Is It? Is It Fair or Raining?

Prove that either A's statement is true and B's and C's are both false, or A's statement is false and B's and C's are both true. Once you have done this—and figured out which of the two alternatives is the case—you are well on your way to a solution.

Who Pilfered the Pies?

Assume Arn's statement is true. What conclusions does this lead to?

Who Stole the Bread?

Examine each statement and, using what you are told, determine which one of the three can be true.

The Missing Meat Pastries

Assume Arn's statement is true; what does that tell you about Con's statement?

The Doughnut Raid

List all the possible pairs of accomplices and use the given facts to eliminate those pairs that could not have made the theft.

A Master Robbery

First determine whether Arn is one of the two thieves.

A Princess or a Dragon? I

Sorry, no hint; any hint would be a giveaway of the answer.

A Princess or a Dragon? II

Focus, first, on the sign on the middle cave.

A Princess or a Dragon? III

Suppose both signs are false. Do you find a contradiction?

A Princess or a Dragon? IV

Suppose the sign on cave A is true. What conclusions do you reach?

Can a Fairy Say "I'm a Green Fairy"?

No hint; any hint would be a giveaway of the answer.

Pink or Green Fairy?

Assume that A is a real green fairy and look for contradictions.

Three Pink or Green Fairies

Consider whether it is possible for A and B to be different types of fairies.

Yellow or Blue? I

Review the logic of disjunction and conjunction (see page 35) if you are at all confused about this area of logic. Then, suppose the fairy's baton is a magic wand. Does that assumption lead to a conclusion about her type? Finally, suppose her baton is an ordinary stick.

Does that assumption lead to a conclusion about her type?

Yellow or Blue? Magic Wand or Not? I

What happens if you assume the fairy's baton is magical?

Yellow or Blue? II

The amazing fact that is exemplified in this puzzle is that if Q is a statement, then any time a fairy says, "If I have a magic wand, then Q," Q must be true, whatever Q is. Can you prove this?

Yellow or Blue? Magic Wand or Not? II

Show that B must be carrying an ordinary stick. Use this fact to prove what kind of fairy B is. We are told that A is the other kind. Then evaluate A's statement knowing what kind she is.

Boots for the Ogres

What if the first three boots the ogre removed were three different colors?

Monster Heads/Monster Feet

I'm afraid this requires algebra, or a lot of trial and error.

King Arthur Meets with King Balfour

Choose the knight for seat #2 first. In how many ways may he be chosen? Now choose the knight for seat #3. He can be chosen in exactly the same number of ways as the knight for seat #2. Once you get to seat #3 you have a more limited number of ways of selecting the knight. How many are left to choose from? Continue from here.

Tending Horses

This puzzle requires some basic algebra. You will have four equations with four "unknowns." (See how helpful algebra can be?)

How Long Did Dob Walk?

Since Alicia and Dob arrived home ten minutes earlier than usual, Alicia drove for ten minutes less than usual. If you cannot come up with a general solution, try doing it by example. For example, you might suppose that Alicia's round trip (cottage to dock) is 60 minutes.

Magical Substance

When will the bowl be half full? Work backwards from this point.

Crossing the River

One of the knights must make the first trip. Who can be left alone with whom or what on this first trip?

The Farmer and the Hobgoblin

Figure out how many coins the farmer had just before the final doubling.

Wizard Rankings

From statement 1, there are two possibilities regarding the ranking changes of Fortuna and Deviner. One of these leads to a contradiction of another clue.

Minotaur Fighters

Start at the end and work toward the first lending.

To the King's Castle

Draw a diagram.

Building a Bridge

First figure out what part of the job Dobbit and Mobbit do in one hour when they work together.

What Time Does the Wagon Driver Leave His Hut?

First, figure out what part of the total trip the driver makes in the 10 minutes from 4:05 to 4:15.

Meeting the Stone Cutter

The cart driver spent 20 minutes less time traveling than he usually did. Of this 20 minutes, half would have been spent going toward the ferry and half coming from the ferry.

The Daughters of Alexis

Ten different combinations of three numbers add to
11, so the first clue is insufficient. You need to figure
out why the next clue still fails to give sufficient
information to Blythe.

How Far from Castleton to Devil's Peak?

Draw a diagram showing each rider's route.

SOLUTIONS

A Master Robbery

The thieves were Birn and Dob. If Arn were one of the thieves, his statement would be false, so Con would be unable to ride and would be innocent. That would mean Con's statement was true; hence, Dob would be guilty. That means Dob's statement would have to be false. But Dob said that either Con was guilty or Arn was guilty, and, since Arn is guilty under our current assumption, Dob's statement would be true. From this contradiction, we know that Arn must be innocent. If Birn is also innocent, then Con and Dob are guilty. But that cannot be true, since Con's statement would be true if Dob is innocent (i.e., this is a contradiction since the two thieves lied). So Birn must be guilty; hence Birn's statement is false. That means Con is innocent and Dob is guilty. (Note: this checks out, since Dob's statement would be untrue and Con's statement would be true.)

In the Forest

Prince Benjamin. We know that Sir Kay shot down more than Princess Paula (statement 1), and that Prince Benjamin captured more than Sir Kay (statement 2). Therefore, Prince Benjamin captured more than either Sir Kay or Princess Paula.

In addition, we know that Princess Paula hit more than Prince Abel (statement 3). Therefore, Prince Benjamin was more successful than Sir Kay, Paula, or Abel.

Captured!

Prince Abel's.

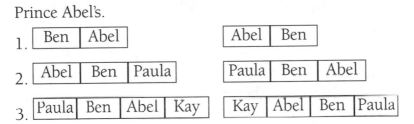

The King's Heir

Both lied.

If you read the puzzle carefully, you'll see that the answer is obvious and that the puzzle doesn't require the involved solution that follows. It is included here only as an easy introduction to the method, which is useful for more difficult puzzles.

	<u>1</u>	<u>2</u>	<u>3</u>	<u>4</u>
Black Hair	T	T	F	F
Red Hair	T	F	T	F

1. The first possibility indicates that both princes were telling the truth. But we were told that at least one of them was lying.

2. We can eliminate both 2 and 3 because if either lied, the other could not have spoken the truth.

   If the prince with black hair lied when he said he was Abel, then he was Benjamin and the other prince must have been Abel. If the prince with red hair lied when he said he was Benjamin, then he must have been Abel and the other prince must have been Benjamin.

3. Therefore, both lied.

Which One Is the Knight?

C is a knight, A is a normal, B is a spy. One of the three is a knight, so C must be telling the truth. If not, then all three individuals are lying, and none could be a knight. Suppose B's statement is true. Then A is a knight. Since knights are always truthful, A's statement would be true: B would be a spy. But that presents us with the contradiction that a spy has made a true statement. So B's statement is untrue. Since C's statement is true, it follows that A's is also. Thus, B is a spy (since A's statement is true) and A is not a knight (since B's statement is false). So A must be a normal. C is, then, the knight.

The First Magic Number

75.

50	51	52	53	54	55	56	57	58	59
60	61	62	63	64	65	66	67	68	69
70	71	72	73	74	75	76	77	78	79

1. Condition A eliminates all multiples of 2 except those from 50 to 59. Eliminated therefore are 60, 62, 64, 66, 68 and 70, 72, 74, 76 and 78.

50	51	52	53	54	55	56	57	58	59
~~60~~	61	~~62~~	63	~~64~~	65	~~66~~	67	~~68~~	69
~~70~~	71	~~72~~	73	~~74~~	75	~~76~~	77	~~78~~	79

2. Condition B indicates that if the number was not a multiple of 3, it was a number from 60 through 69. This eliminates 50, 52, 53, 55, 56, 58, 59 and 71, 73, 77 and 79.

~~50~~	51	~~52~~	~~53~~	54	~~55~~	~~56~~	57	~~58~~	~~59~~
~~60~~	61	~~62~~	63	~~64~~	65	~~66~~	67	~~68~~	69
~~70~~	~~71~~	~~72~~	~~73~~	~~74~~	75	~~76~~	~~77~~	~~78~~	~~79~~

3. Condition C indicates that if the number was not a multiple of 4, then it was a number from 70 through 79. This eliminates 51, 54, 57 and 61, 63, 65, 67 and 69.

~~50~~	~~51~~	~~52~~	~~53~~	~~54~~	~~55~~	~~56~~	~~57~~	~~58~~	~~59~~
~~60~~	~~61~~	~~62~~	~~63~~	~~64~~	~~65~~	~~66~~	~~67~~	~~68~~	~~69~~
~~70~~	~~71~~	~~72~~	~~73~~	~~74~~	75	~~76~~	~~77~~	~~78~~	~~79~~

4. The remaining number, 75, satisfies all three conditions.

   A. It is not a multiple of 2 and so it does not have to be a number from 50 through 59.

   B. It is a multiple of 3, and so it does not have to be a number from 60 through 69.

   C. It is not a multiple of 4, and so it is, necessarily, a number from 70 through 79.

The Missing Swords

C. Number and direction are involved. There are three sets of single swords, three sets of double swords, but only two sets of three swords. None of the swords points downward.

The Ogre's Boast

100 or none.

	A	**B**	**C**	**D**	**E**	**F**	**G**	**H**
Ogre	T	T	T	T	F	F	F	F
Kay	T	T	F	F	T	T	F	F
Abel	T	F	F	T	T	F	T	F

1. We can eliminate possibilities A, B, D, and E, because they indicate that two of the statements are true, and we are told that only one statement is true.

2. We can eliminate H, because it indicates that all the statements are false, and we know that one is true.

3. That leaves three possibilities: C, F, and G.

	C	**F**	**G**
Ogre	T	F	F
Kay	F	T	F
Abel	F	F	T

4. If the ogre's claim that he devoured more than 100 is true, then Sir Kay's statement that the ogre ate *fewer* than 100 is false. But Abel's statement that the ogre ate at least one *can't* be false. So C is eliminated.

5. G need not be contradictory. Suppose the ogre's boast of more than 100 and Sir Kay's statement of less than 100 are false. Abel's statement that the ogre ate at least one could be true—if the ogre ate exactly 100.

6. As for F: if Sir Kay's statement that the ogre devoured fewer than 100 is true, then the ogre's claim is false. And Abel's statement that the ogre devoured at least one could also be false—if the ogre ate none!

Name the Knights

#1 is Black; #2 is Pure; #3 is Good; #4 is Glory; #5 is Bad; #6 is Grand; #7 is Noble; #8 is Brave; #9 is Chaste; #10 is White. From the preceding puzzle, we know that #1, #5, and #7 were the three knights who won one or more contests. From clues 1, 2, and 4, these three knights were, in some order, Sir Black,

Sir Noble, and Sir Bad. The other seven knights were Sir Pure, Sir Brave, Sir Good, Sir Grand, Sir Chaste, Sir White, and Sir Glory. Sir Good's single contest was four matches before that between Sir Noble and Sir Bad (clue 3). Since both Sir Noble and Sir Bad won one or more contests, they have to have been #5 and #7 in one or the other order. Either way, Sir Good must have been #3, and Sir Black must have been #1 (previous puzzle's solution). Sir Noble defeated Sir Brave in Sir Brave's only contest (clue 2). Suppose Sir Noble had been #5 and Sir Bad #7. Then Sir Brave would have been #6. That would mean two knights whose names begin with "B" had consecutive numbers assigned to them (i.e., Sir Brave would have been #6, and Sir Bad would have been #7), contradicting clue 6. So Sir Noble was #7, Sir Bad was #5, and Sir Brave was not #6. Sir Brave was either #8 or #9 (clue 2). He can't have been #9, as then clue 5 couldn't be met. So Sir Brave was #8, whence, by clue 5, we know that Sir Chaste was #9 and Sir White was #10. Sir Bad defeated Sir Grand (clue 4), so, since Sir Grand won no contests, Sir Grand was #6. Sir Glory, then, was #4 (clue 7). By elimination, Sir Pure was #2.

The Second Magic Number

64. (See First Magic Number solution, page 109, for how-to-solve example.)

The Third Magic Number

44. (See First Magic Number solution, page 109, for how-to-solve example.)

Who Stole the Bread?

Con is the thief. If Arn were the thief, his statement would be true, contradicting the fact that the thief lied. So Arn's statement is false, and Arn is not the thief. This means that Birn told the truth when he said that Arn was lying. So Birn is not the thief. By elimination, Con is the thief (and he lied when he identified Birn as the thief).

The New Year's Eve Ball

First: Sir Good, white; second: Sir Venerable, blue; third: Sir Pure, gold; fourth: Sir Pious, purple. By clue 1, the four knights were Sir Pious, the knight who arrived second, the knight whose horse wore white trappings, and Sir Pure. These facts may be entered into a chart as shown on page 115.

Knights	**Order of Arrival**	**Color**
1. Pious		
2.	2nd	
3.		white
4. Pure		

Since Sir Venerable's steed did not wear white trappings (clue 3), Sir Venerable must be the knight who arrived second. Thus, Sir Good rode the horse with white trappings. We now have:

Knights	**Order of Arrival**	**Color**
1. Pious		
2. Venerable	2nd	
3. Good		white
4. Pure		

By clue 2, Sir Pious arrived fourth. Sir Good did not arrive third (clue 4), so he arrived first, and the horse with blue trappings was Sir Venerable's mount (also clue 4). Sir Pure arrived third (process of elimination). By clue 5, the horse with purple trappings wasn't ridden by Sir Pure, so it was Sir Pious's mount. Finally, the horse wearing gold trappings carried Sir Pure (process of elimination).

The Wizard Waves a Wand

C. Each dragon and knight moves to the left.

Merlin and the Disguises

Sir Good was disguised as Sir Kay, Sir Kay as Alt, Alt as Maj, Maj as Merlin, Merlin as Sir Good. We are told that each of the five was disguised as one of the other four, and that no two of the five were disguised as the same person. First, we determine which person was disguised as Merlin. That person was not Alt (clue 3). Suppose he had been Sir Good. Then, by clue 1, Merlin would have been disguised as Alt, so that, by clue 2, Alt would have been disguised as Sir Kay. But this would mean (clue 3) that Sir Kay as well as Sir Good portrayed Merlin. So we have a contradiction of what we are told. By similar reasoning, it was not Sir Kay who portrayed Merlin. For if it had been, then, by clue 3, Alt would have portrayed Sir Kay, so that, by clue 2, Merlin would have been disguised as Alt, and, by clue 1, Sir Good as well as Sir Kay would have been disguised as Merlin. By elimination, it was the squire Maj who was disguised as Merlin. So Alt was disguised as Maj (clue 3), and the person who was disguised as Alt was not Sir Good (clue 1). Suppose that person had been Merlin. Then Alt would have been disguised as Sir Kay as well as Maj (clue 2), a contradiction. So it was Sir Kay who was disguised as Alt. Thus, by clue 1, it was Sir Good who portrayed Sir Kay. By elimination (or by clue 2), Merlin had to be disguised as Sir Good.

Who Won the Jousting Tournament?

Exactly three knights won one or more contests (clue 1). The first contest was between #1 and #2, so either #1 or #2 won at least one contest. A second winner was #5, since in order to have contested #6 (clue 2), #5 would have to have defeated a prior opponent. The third winner was #7, since #7 must have defeated #8 in order to have contested #9 (clue 3). By the rules and what we have deduced thus far, we know that #3 and #4 won no contests. Both were defeated by the same knight, either #1 or #2. By clue 4, that knight was #1. So #1 defeated #2, #3, and #4 in order. Then, since clue 2 tells us that one contest was between #5 and #6, it follows that #1 lost when he fought #5. So the three winners of one or more matches were #1, #5, and #7.

Thus, #5 must have defeated #6, only to have been overcome by #7, who must have gone on to defeat, in turn, numbers 8, 9, and 10, to win the tournament.

In summary, in the order of the matches:

> #1 defeated #2, #3, and #4 in succession
> #5 defeated #1 and #6 in succession
> #7 defeated, in order, #5, #8, #9, and #10

What Day of the Week Is It? I

Sunday. If it were Tuesday, Thursday, or Saturday, days on which the inhabitant always tells the truth, he would not lie and say he had told the truth on the previous day. If it were Monday, Wednesday, or Friday, days on which he always lies, he would not say he had told the truth on the previous day — for such a statement would be true. It is Sunday, a day on which the inhabitant tells the truth, and the only day of the week on which it is true that he tells the truth on the preceding day.

Can a Fairy Say, "I'm a Green Fairy"?

No. If the pink-looking fairy were a real pink fairy, she would tell the truth and would not say that she is a green fairy, and if she were really a green fairy, she would not truthfully say that she was.

A Princess or a Dragon?   IV

Caves B and C contain the princesses. Suppose the sign on cave A is true, so that cave B contains a dragon. Then the sign on cave B is false (because cave B contains a dragon), and so cave C contains a dragon (because the sign on B, which, under our assumption, is false, says that cave C does not contain a dragon). Then, since cave C contains a dragon, the sign on cave C must be false; but that is a contradiction, since, under our assumption that the statement on cave A is true, cave B contains a dragon.

So, we have shown that the sign on cave A must be false. Therefore, cave B contains a princess, and thus it bears a sign with a true statement. Since the statement on cave B is true, it follows that cave C contains a princess and bears a sign with a true statement (which checks out, since, from what we are told, the second dragon must be in cave D; note that the sign on cave D is false, which checks out, since cave C does not contain a dragon).

The Pavilions of the Champions

A: Sir Good, oak tree, Hab; B: Sir Chaste, lion, Bran; C: Sir Pure, bear, Col; D: Sir Brave, falcon, Altur; E: Sir White, dragon, Fel. By clue 3, pavilion C belonged to the knight whose emblem was the bear. By clue 4, Sir White's pavilion was E, Altur was the squire at pavilion D, and the oak tree was the emblem of the knight at pavilion A. Bran was the squire at B (clue 5). By clue 6, the knight at D had the emblem of the falcon. Sir Chaste had pavilion B (clue 9). Sir Brave's pavilion was not C (clue 1) or A (clue 2), so Sir Brave had pavilion D. Col's knight had pavilion C (clue 1). Since Fel's knight did not have pavilion A (clue 5), Fel's knight had pavilion E, and Hab's knight, by elimination, had pavilion A. By clue 7, the lion was not Sir White's emblem, so the knight whose emblem was the lion had pavilion B, and the dragon, by elimination, was the emblem of pavilion E's knight. By clue 8, Sir Good's pavilion was A. By elimination, Sir Pure's was C.

Knights, Normals, and Spies I

A is the knight, B is the spy, C is the normal. We know that exactly one of the three is a knight and one a spy. The knight can't be C since, if C were a knight, his statement would be a true statement; therefore, B would also be a knight. Now, suppose B is the knight. Then C's statement would be true, so C would not be the spy, exactly what A said. So A's statement would be true also, so none of the three could be a spy, contrary to what we are told. So B is not the knight. A must be the knight. Now B's statement is false, and as B is not a knight, C's statement is false. But, from A's statement, C is not a spy, so C is the normal, and B is the spy.

A Princess or a Dragon? I

Cave A does not contain a dragon; cave B does. One of the signs is false and the other true. Since one of the caves contains a dragon, the sign on cave A is necessarily true. Since only one of the signs is true, the one on cave B is false. The dragon, then, is in cave B.

Three Pink or Green Fairies

A and B are pink; C is green; A appears to be green. We show that A and B must be the same kind of fairy (in essence, that is—not necessarily in appearance). Suppose they are two different types. First, suppose A is pink and B is green. This cannot be the case, because if A were a pink fairy, she would not make the false statement that B is pink. Now, suppose A is green and B is pink. This cannot be the case either, because if A were a green fairy, she would not make the true statement that B is pink. So A and B are either both pink fairies or both green fairies. Suppose they are both green. Then A is green, so the "if" part of B's statement ("A is a pink fairy") is false. This means (recalling the discussion of logical implication) that B's statement is true, a contradiction of the assumption that B is a green fairy. So both A and B are pink fairies. Therefore, since A is a pink fairy and B has made a true "if-then" statement, it follows that C is a green fairy.

Then, remembering what it means for an "or" statement to be false, we know that both parts of C's statement are false (since C is green). Hence, "A is what she appears to be" is a false statement. So A must appear to be green.

The Three Suspects

We show that if A had said that he was a knight, the judge would not have been able to positively identify a spy among the three prisoners. In this case, any one of the three could be a spy. The first prisoner could be a spy and either one of the others could be a knight. The second prisoner could be a spy if the first is a knight and the third a normal (lying on this occasion). The third prisoner could be a spy and either the first or second a knight. So A must have said, "I'm a normal." Now if A's statement is true, he is a normal, so both B's and C's statements would be false, and we would be left with no knight among the three. So A's statement must be false; he is not a normal, but he lied, so he must be a spy. So B's and C's statements are both true. The judge could not have known which of B and C was a knight and which was a normal, but of course, the judge has done his duty by determining that A is the only spy.

What Day of the Week Is It? II

Friday. Clearly these statements were not made on
Sunday, the one day of the week on which all of the
inhabitants tell the truth. On any other day of the week,
one of the inhabitants tells the truth and the other lies,
so one statement must be true and the other one false.
Suppose A's statement is the true statement; then
yesterday was Sunday, and today is Monday. But A lies
on Mondays, so this cannot be the case. So A's statement
is false. Thus, B's statement is true: tomorrow is Saturday
and today is Friday. (B tells the truth on Fridays and A
lies on Fridays, so there is no contradiction.)

A Lame Horse

10 times. The knight walked two-thirds of the
distance and rode one-third of it, so he walked twice
as far as he rode. The walking portion took twenty
times as long as the riding portion; so, if the walking
and riding distances had been the same, the walking
part would have taken ten times as long as the riding
part. Thus, the knight rode ten times as fast as he
walked.

Who Pilfered the Pies?

Arn is definitely guilty. Assume Arn's statement is the one of the three that is true. Then Arn is not guilty, so both Birn and Con are guilty. But that means that both Birn's and Con's statements would be true. This is a contradiction of what we are told (i.e., that just one of the three statements is true). So Arn's statement is false. Therefore Arn is guilty. Attempts to discover whether Birn or Con is the other guilty one are unfruitful. If the one true statement were made by Birn, then Con is guilty, and if it were made by Con, Birn is guilty. Since we do not have a way to determine which one of the two made the true statement, we cannot determine whether it is Birn or Con who is the other thief.

Knights, Normals, and Spies II

A is the normal, B is the spy, C is the knight. A knight would not say that he is a normal, so B cannot be the knight. Nor can B be the normal, for then B's statement would be true, whence both A's and C's would also be true—a contradiction since at least one of the statements is false (the one made by the spy). So B is the spy, and his statement is false. Thus, A's statement is false, so A is the normal of the three. Finally, C is the knight (the "his statement is false" part of C's statement is true, making the entire statement true).

Monster Heads/Monster Feet

30 of the monsters with two heads and three feet each, 20 of the others. This puzzle is most easily solved by using algebra. If x = the number of monsters with two heads and three feet each, and y = the number of monsters with three heads and four feet each, then, from the given facts we have:

(1) $2x + 3y = 120$
(2) $3x + 4y = 170$

Now multiply each member of the first equation by 3 and each member of the second by -2 and add together the resulting equivalent equations, as follows, to obtain $y = 20$:

$$
\begin{array}{lrr}
(1a) & 6x + 9y = & 360 \\
(2a) & -6x - 8y = & -340 \\
& y = & 20
\end{array}
$$

Since y = 20, we have, from the original equation 1,
2x + 3(20) = 120, 2x + 60 = 12, 2x = 60, x = 30.

Feeding the Horses

Yes. Sixty-nine days of winter remain, and enough
food is on hand to feed the two remaining horses for
72 days. This puzzle can be solved using algebra, but I
like the following solution: When the four horses were
sold, Distal had been feeding his original six horses for
6 days. Had he kept all six horses, he would have been
able to feed them for another 24 days. But as he had
only two horses—one-third as many—the food will
last three times as long, or 72 days.

Yellow or Blue, Magic Wand or Not? I

Yellow fairy/ordinary stick. If she were carrying a magic
wand her statement would be true, so both parts would
be true (The "I am carrying an ordinary stick" part as
well as the "I am a blue fairy" part). This can't be the
case, so she must be carrying an ordinary stick. Thus,
her (compound) statement is false, which means one
or the other part of it is false, or both parts are false.

We know that the "I am carrying an ordinary stick" part is true, so it must be false that she is a blue fairy; so she is a yellow fairy.

The Genie and the Coins

A. Double the number of coins in the preceding box and add 1 (2 + 1 = 3, 6+ 1 = 7, 14 + 1 = 15, 30 + 1 = 31).

Chased by a Glub

Since Phipos first ran for half the time it took him to reach the fort, he ran for more than half the distance. So, when half the distance had been covered, Phipos was still running, but the glub had begun to walk. Therefore, the glub fell farther and farther behind Phipos. When Phipos began to walk, the glub was still walking, so the distance Phipos gained while he ran and the glub walked was maintained.

What Day of the Week Is It? III

Monday. From puzzle 5, we know that if A were a Monday–Wednesday–Friday liar, he could make the statement, "I told the truth yesterday," only on a Sunday.

However, if A were a Tuesday–Thursday–Saturday liar, he could have made his statement only on Monday. So either:

A is a Monday–Wednesday–Friday liar and spoke on Sunday, *or*

A is a Tuesday–Thursday–Saturday liar and spoke on Monday.

If B were a Monday–Wednesday–Friday liar, he could have said "Yesterday was Monday" on a Monday, a Wednesday, or a Friday because the statement would have been a lie on those days. Or, he could have said it on a Tuesday, because the statement would be true on a day when he tells the truth. On the other hand, if B were a Tuesday–Thursday–Saturday liar, he could have made the statement "Yesterday was Monday" only on a Thursday or Saturday, the only days on which it is a fact both that he lies and that the statement is a lie. He couldn't have made it on a Monday, Wednesday, or Friday because the statement would be false on a day when he tells the truth. So, either:

B is a Monday–Wednesday–Friday liar and spoke on Monday, Tuesday, Wednesday, or Friday, *or*

B is a Tuesday–Thursday–Saturday liar and spoke on Thursday or Saturday.

We seek a day of the week on which both statements could be made, one by one type of liar and the second by the other type. Obviously the only day that could work would be Monday, if A is a Tuesday–Thursday–Saturday liar and B a Monday–Wednesday–Friday liar.

The Missing Meat Pastries

Arn is guilty. If Arn's statement is the one that is true, then Arn is innocent (since only one of the three is the thief), so Con's statement is true also. We cannot have two true statements, so Arn's statement is false. Since the content of Arn's statement is false, neither Birn nor Con is guilty, and Arn is. The one who made a true statement is Birn.

Yellow or Blue? I

Blue fairy (it cannot be determined whether she carries a magic wand or an ordinary stick). Suppose the fairy's baton is a magic wand. Then, because she carries a magic wand we know her statement is true, meaning that at least one part is true:

"I am a blue fairy and I have a magic wand" is true, or

"I am a yellow fairy and I have an ordinary stick"
is true.

The second part is false, because we have assumed
she is carrying a magic wand. So the first part is true;
she is a blue fairy.

Now suppose the fairy is carrying an ordinary stick.
Then, because she is carrying an ordinary stick, her
statement is false. This means both parts of her statement
are false: she is not a blue fairy with a magic wand, and
she is not a yellow fairy with an ordinary stick. Since she
does have an ordinary stick, it is obvious she is not a
blue fairy with a magic wand. But since she also is not a
"yellow fairy with an ordinary stick," she must be a blue
fairy with an ordinary stick, as that is the only way the
statement, "I am a yellow fairy and I am carrying an
ordinary stick" can be false.

The Doughnut Raid

The thieves are Birn and Dob. The two were not Arn
and Con, or Arn and Dob (statement 1), or Birn and
Cob (statement 2), or Arn and Birn (statement 3), or
Con and Dob (statement 4). By elimination, they were
Birn and Dob.

Weighing a Pound of Flour

She put the one-pound weight on one pan of the scale and balanced it with lead pellets placed on the other pan. She then removed the one-pound weight and replaced it with flour until it balanced the lead pellets.

A Princess or a Dragon? III

Both caves contains princesses. Suppose both signs bore false statements. Then, by the false statement on cave B, cave A contains a dragon. But that means that the statement on cave A is true, a contradiction. So both signs have true statements on them. By the true statement on cave B, cave A contains a princess. By the true sign on cave A, cave B contains a princess.

Boots for the Ogres

Eight. If the first three boots removed from the chest happened to be three different colors, then a fourth boot must be removed to obtain the first pair of boots of the same color. Assume this is the case, and assume, without loss of generality, that the fourth boot is black. The boots removed at this point would be: one white boot, one brown boot, one pair (two) black boots. Then, suppose that the fifth boot is black, which could be the case, since there are three boots of each color in the chest. Thus, the first five boots removed from the chest would consist of: one white boot, one brown boot, three black boots. So a sixth boot would have to be removed in order to guarantee a second pair. Since the three black boots have all been removed, the sixth boot would have to be either white or brown. Without loss of generality, assume it is brown. So the boots removed to this point would consist of: 3 black boots, 2 brown boots, one white boot. Then, if the seventh boot happened to be brown, the boots removed at this point would be: 3 black boots, 3 brown boots, one white boot. Thus, an eighth boot would have to be removed in order to obtain a third pair of matching boots—which, of course, under our without-loss-of-generality assumptions, would be white.

Pink or Green Fairy?

A is as she appears to be, a pink fairy; B is really a green fairy. Suppose A is a green fairy. Then A's statement is a lie, so B is a pink fairy. This leads us to the contradiction that B is a pink fairy who has made a false statement. So A must be a pink fairy. Therefore, A's statement that B is a green fairy is true (which checks out without contradiction, since B's statement is false).

How Long Did Dob Walk?

55 minutes. Since Alicia and Dob arrived home ten minutes earlier than usual, Alicia drove ten minutes less than usual. So she drove one way—towards the ferry dock—for five minutes less than usual. Had she driven for the other five minutes, she would have arrived at the ferry dock at the usual time, one hour later than Dob's actual time of arrival on this particular day. So Dob must have walked for 55 minutes. If you don't understand this, don't be dismayed. It is not an easy problem.

Let's look at an example, just to convince you that 55 minutes is the correct answer. Suppose that the time required for one round trip for Alicia is 60 minutes (30 minutes each way). Also, without loss of generality, suppose that she usually leaves the cottage at 6:00, thus arriving at the ferry dock at 6:30 and arriving back home with Dob at 7:00. On the day in question, she leaves at her usual time, 6:00, but she and Dob arrive home at 6:50. Dob arrived at the ferry dock at 5:30 and began walking. Alicia's total round-trip time is 50 minutes, so she drove the mule for 25 minutes before she met Dob. She left home at 6:00 and met Dob at 6:25. Dob had been walking since 5:30, a total of 55 minutes. Try this with a different set of assumptions and you will still arrive at 55 minutes for an answer.

How Many Cakes?

24 cakes; each being took 6. Heartnik took ¼ the original number, leaving ¾ of that number. Scowler took ⅓ of that ¾, or ¼ of the original number. So, after Heartnik and Scowler had helped themselves, ½ the original number of cakes remained on the plate. Goodin took ½ of that half, so he, as well as Heartnik and Scowler, took ¼ of the original number. Thus, after Goodin had helped himself, ¼ the original number remained. So Loglob, the last being to take the cakes, took ¼ the original number. As he took six cakes, there were 24 cakes in the beginning, and each being took six.

Crossing the River

Sir Good rows the corn over, leaves it, and rows back alone. Then Sir Pure rows the ogre over, leaves the ogre with the corn, and rows back alone. Sir Good and Sir Pure then row over together (leaving the goose behind). Sir Pure stays with the corn and the ogre. Sir Good rows back, picks up the goose, and rows across the river.

Genie Horseplay

B. The horse immediately to the left of the genie grows. The horse to the immediate right of the genie shrinks.

Yellow or Blue? II

Yellow. Suppose that the fairy carries a magic wand. Then the statement, "If I have a magic wand, I am a yellow fairy," must be true (since fairies with magic wands always tell the truth). So the "then" part of her statement would be true: she would be a yellow fairy. Therefore, it is proved that if she carries a magic wand she is a yellow fairy. But that is precisely what she asserted. Therefore, she made a true statement, so she must carry a magic wand. And since we have proved that if she carries a magic wand she is yellow, then it must be true that she is yellow.

Building a Bridge

15 hours. For each hour that Dobbit worked, $\frac{1}{30}$ of the project was completed. So after Dobbit had worked 5 hours alone, $5(\frac{1}{30})$, or $\frac{1}{6}$, of the job was completed, leaving $\frac{5}{6}$ of the job for Dobbit and Mobbit to do together. For each hour that Mobbit worked, he did $\frac{1}{45}$ of the job. For each hour the two worked together, the part of the job that was done was $\frac{1}{30} + \frac{1}{45} = \frac{5}{90}$, which reduces to $\frac{1}{18}$. So, together, the two would do the entire job in 18 hours. Thus, to do $\frac{5}{6}$ of it required $\frac{5}{6} \times 18 = 15$ hours.

How Can Everyone Cross the River?

The half-elf rows the human across to Tok, leaving the dwarf and the elf at Ak. The half-elf leaves the human at Tok and returns to Ak alone. On his next trip the half-elf rows the dwarf across, leaving the elf alone at

Ak. The half-elf leaves the dwarf in Tok and returns to Ak with the human. Leaving the human at Ak, the half-elf rows the elf across the river and leaves the elf with the dwarf at Tok. On the last trip the half-elf takes the human across again to Tok.

Tending Horses

The puzzle can best be solved by using algebra. If we let a = the number of mares Aken tends, b = the number of mares Col tends, c = the number of stallions Aken tends, and d = the number of stallions Col tends, we obtain four equations in four unknowns:

(1)   b = 2a
(2)   c = 4a
(3)   c = d + 2
(4)   d = b + 2

Using the fact that b = 2a (equation 1), by substitution of 2a for b in equation 4, we obtain:

(5)   d = 2a + 2

From equation 2, c = 4a, so substituting 4a for c in equation 3, we obtain:

(6)   4a = d + 2

Equation 6 may also be written:

(7)   d = 4a − 2

Then, by substitution, using equations 5 and 7, we obtain: 2a + 2 = 4a − 2. Then, by arithmetic, 2a = 4, so a = 2. The rest is obtained by substitution. Since a = 2, b = 4 (equation 1). Since a = 2, c = 8 (equation 2). Since b = 4, d = 6 (equation 4).

The Farmer and the Hobgoblin

15 coins. To solve the puzzle, start at the end. Since the farmer gave the hobgoblin his "last sixteen coins," sixteen is the number of coins the farmer had after the final doubling; so, he had eight coins when he crossed the field for the last time. Add to this the sixteen he gave the hobgoblin after the third crossing, and the result is twenty-four, which is twice the number of coins he had before the third crossing.

So the farmer had twelve coins when he started the third crossing. Adding to twelve coins the sixteen he gave the hobgoblin after the second crossing gives twenty-eight coins, which is twice the number he had before the second crossing.

So he started the second crossing with fourteen coins. Add to fourteen the sixteen coins he gave the hobgoblin after the first crossing, and the result is thirty, which is twice the number of coins he started with. Thus, the farmer began the first crossing with fifteen coins.

Yellow or Blue, Magic Wand or Not? II

A is a yellow fairy carrying an ordinary stick; B is a blue fairy carrying an ordinary stick. B cannot be carrying a magic wand, for if so she would be a "truther," hence wouldn't say she is carrying an ordinary stick. So B is carrying an ordinary stick, which means B always lies. Since it's true that she carries an ordinary stick, the only way she can be lying is if she is a blue fairy. Now consider A. Since the two fairies are of different colors, A is a yellow fairy. Since A is a yellow fairy, her statement that she is a blue fairy carrying a magic wand is false. Then, since she made a false statement, she must be carrying an ordinary stick (since fairies with magic wands do not make false statements). Looking at the analysis with respect to A in another way: knowing that A is a yellow fairy, could a yellow fairy with a magic

wand have made the statement A made? Clearly the
answer is "No." Hence, A has an ordinary stick.

What Day of the Week Is It?
Is It Fair or Raining?

It is a clear Saturday. It cannot be a Sunday, clear or
rainy, since A tells the truth on Sunday, whereas, "It is
raining and today is Tuesday" is only true on a rainy
Tuesday. So, since the three statements were made on
a day other than Sunday, either A's statement is true
(it's a rainy Tuesday) and both B's and C's are false, or
A's statement is false and both B's and C's are true.
Now, A's statement cannot be true, for then B's would
also be true (because the "It is Tuesday" portion of it
would be true. Therefore, A's statement is false, and
both B's and C's are true. Any false statement made by
A was made on a fair Tuesday, Thursday, or Saturday,
or on a rainy Monday, Wednesday, or Friday. Any true
statement made by B was made on a fair Tuesday,
Thursday, or Saturday, or on a rainy Monday,
Wednesday, or Friday. But, since B's statement is
known to be true as to its content, it could not have
been made on a rainy Monday, Wednesday, or Friday.

So B's statement was made, and A's statement was made, on a fair Tuesday, Thursday, or Saturday. The only one of those days on which C's statement is true, as it must be, is a clear Saturday (on a clear Tuesday, his statement would be false because tomorrow would be Wednesday, while on a clear Thursday, it would be false because the previous day was Wednesday).

How Much Did Alaranthus Weigh?

3000 pounds. Alaranthus's weight was such that 1000 pounds was equal to one-third of his weight. So his total weight in pounds was 3×1000.

Wizard Rankings

The latest rankings are: 1. Chameleoner, 2. Alchemerion, 3. Elvira, 4. Fortuna, 5. Bogara, 6. Deviner.

From statement 2, either Fortuna's ranking changed from 6 to 2 and Deviner's from 4 to 3, or Fortuna changed from 6 to 4 and Deviner from 4 to 6. If the former were the actual case, then Fortuna's change would have been a four-step change. But Bogara's ranking could not have changed by more than four steps, so a four-step change in Fortuna's ranking would lead to a contradiction of statement 1. So Fortuna's ranking changed from 6 to 4 and Deviner's from 4 to 6.

From statement 1, Bogara's ranking changed from 2 to 5, a three-step change. Since Elvira's change in ranking was smaller than Bogara's, her ranking only changed to 3. All the rankings changed; therefore, Alchemerion's new ranking was 2 and Chameleoner, by elimination, went to the top spot, ranking 1.

How Far Apart Were the Dragons?

5 miles. To solve this puzzle, the formula d = rt (distance = rate multiplied by time) is used. The dragons' rates are stated in miles per hour, so time must be expressed in terms of hours in order to obtain a meaningful answer. Five minutes = $\frac{1}{12}$ hour, so the distance Argothel walked in 5 minutes at a rate of 24 miles per hour was 2 miles ($24 \times \frac{1}{12}$), while Bargothel walked 3 miles ($36 \times \frac{1}{12}$). So the dragons were 5 miles apart 5 minutes before they met.

A Round-Table Arrangement

1, Hob; 2, Rob; 3, Cob; 4, Bob; 5, Tob; 6, Lob.

Cob doesn't have seat #1 (clue 3). From clue 2, either Hob or Lob has that seat. Suppose it is Lob who has the #1 seat. Then Hob would have the #6 seat and Cob the #4 seat (clue 2). Rob would then have seat #3 (clue 3), and Bob would have the #5 seat (clue 1). By elimination, Tob would have seat #2, contradicting clue 4.

So Hob must have seat #1. Cob and Lob have seats #3 and #6, in one order or the other (clue 2). Suppose Lob has seat #3 and Cob seat #6. Then, by clue 1, Bob would have seat #5, while by clue 3, Rob would have seat #5. Thus, Cob has seat #3 and Lob seat #6. By clue 3, Rob has seat #2. Bob has seat #4 (clue 1). By elimination, Tob has seat #5.

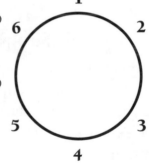

What Time Does the Wagon Driver Leave His Hut?

The driver leaves his hut at 3:50 P.M. and arrives at the dock at 5:05 P.M. In the 10 minutes from 4:05 to 4:15, he goes $\frac{1}{3} - \frac{1}{5} = \frac{2}{15}$ the distance. So in 5 minutes, he goes $\frac{1}{15}$ the distance, and in 15 ($15 \times 5 = 75$) minutes he goes the full distance. At 4:15 he has made $\frac{1}{3}$ of the trip, which has taken $\frac{1}{3}(75) = 25$ minutes. So he leaves his hut at 3:50 and arrives at the dock 75 minutes later, at 5:05.

Magical Substance

$\frac{1}{8}$ full. At the end of the third day, the bowl is half full (since it doubles its volume each day). So at the end of the second day it is $\frac{1}{4}$ full (since $2 \times \frac{1}{4} = \frac{1}{2}$ at the end of the third day). Thus, at the end of the first day it is $\frac{1}{8}$ full (since $2 \times \frac{1}{8} = \frac{1}{4}$ at the end of the second day).

How Far From Castleton to Devil's Peak?

Castleton and Devil's Peak are 10 miles apart. The rider who started his journey at Devil's Peak rode $1\frac{1}{2}$ times as fast as the rider who started his trip at Castleton.

The diagram below shows that when the horsemen met for the first time, they had, together, traveled a distance equal to the distance between Castleton and Devil's Peak. When they met for the second time, they had traveled, together, three times the distance between the two towns.

Both riders traveled at a constant speed, so when they met the second time, each had ridden three times as far as he had when the two met the first time. The rider who began at Castleton had thus traveled 3 × 4 = 12 miles. The distance of 12 miles is 2 miles more than the distance between the towns, so the towns are 10 miles apart.

As for the two riders' relative speed, during the time that the rider who began the trip at Castleton rode 4 miles, the other rider rode 6 miles. So the other rider rode 1½ times as fast.

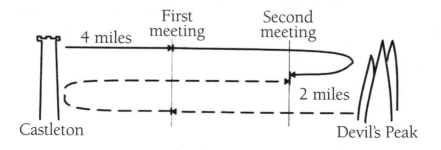

Meeting the Stone Cutter

5:50 A.M. The cart would normally have arrived at the ferry landing at 6:00 A.M. But on the day in question, the cart driver delivered the stone worker to the quarry 20 minutes early, so the driver spent 20 minutes less time traveling than he usually did: 10 minutes going toward the ferry and 10 minutes going to the quarry. Subtract 10 minutes from 6:00 A.M. to get 5:50 A.M., the time the cart met the worker.

If you find this difficult to follow, let's say that normally the driver leaves the quarry at 5:00 A.M. in order to arrive at the ferry at 6:00 A.M. and deliver the worker to the quarry at 7:00 A.M. In other words the cart driver drives one hour each way on a normal day. But on the day in question, the cart driver delivered the worker to the quarry at 6:40. The cart driver left for the ferry at his usual time, 5:00 A.M., and drove until 6:40, so he drove for 100 minutes—50 minutes in one direction and 50 in another. Normally he drives 60 minutes to reach the ferry landing. Thus, he drove for 10 fewer minutes toward the ferry landing. So he must have picked up the worker at 5:50 A.M. rather than 6:00 A.M.

How Did the Archers Cross the River?

First, the two children rowed the boat across. One child remained on the river's far side while the second child rowed back to the archers. An archer then rowed across alone. This archer sent the boat back with the child who had remained on the far side of the river. The two children then rowed across again, and again one remained on the far side while the other rowed back. Next, a second archer rowed across, and sent the boat back with the child who had been left on the far side of the river. This process was repeated until all the archers were across.

How Early Was the Barge?

20 minutes early. The cart driver traveled 24 minutes less than usual. If he had not met the rider, he would have needed half of those minutes, 12 minutes, to get to the dock at his usual time. But the rider had ridden for 8 minutes before he and the cart driver met, so the barge was 12 + 8 = 20 minutes early.

The Sons of Blythe

They are 2, 3, and 6 years old. Since all three are younger than 10 years of age, and the product of the ages of the two youngest equals the age of the oldest, the ages are 2, 2, 4; or 2, 3, 6; or 2, 4, 8; or 3, 3, 9. Of these, only 2, 3, and 6 add up to a number that is a prime number.

The Human Population of South Pymm

389. The population of North Pymm is smaller than 500 and is a number that has 3, 4, 5 and 7 as integral factors (i.e., 3, 4, 5, and 7 divide into the number without a remainder). Since 3, 4, 5, and 7 are relatively prime, the smallest possible number is the product of 3, 4, 5, and 7, which is 420. The next largest possible number would be 840, which is too large. So the population of North Pymm is 420 and the population of South Pymm is ($\frac{1}{3}$) 420 + ($\frac{1}{4}$) 420 + ($\frac{1}{5}$) 420 + ($\frac{1}{7}$) 420 = 140 + 105 + 84 + 60 = 389.

Measuring Two Gallons of Cider

Fill the 3-gallon container with cider and empty it into the 4-gallon container. Fill the 3-gallon container a second time and pour it into the 4-gallon container. When the 4-gallon container is full, 2 gallons remain in the 3-gallon container.

Rings for the Princesses

King Firnal can bestow two princesses with rings and then give the box with the remaining ring to the third princess.

The Daughters of Alexis

The girls are 1, 2, and 8 years old. Blythe could not answer the question using the first clue because ten different combinations of three numbers add up to 11 (1, 1, 9; 1, 2, 8; 1, 3, 7; 1, 4, 6; 1, 5, 5; 2, 2, 7; 2, 3, 6; 2, 4, 5; 3, 3, 5; 3, 4, 4).

Since the second clue did not provide Blythe with the answer, it must be the case that at least two combinations from the list above have a product which is either 16 years more or 16 years less than Blythe's age. The products derived from the list above are, in the order of the list, 9, 16, 21, 24, 25, 28, 36, 40, 45, 48. Since no two of these products are the same, it must be true that one product is 16 more and the other is 16 less than Blythe's age. Thus, the difference between these two products is 32.

Comparing each product with each of the others, we find two products that meet this requirement: 16 and 48, the products of 1, 2, and 8, and 3, 4, and 4, respectively (thus, Blythe is 32 years old). Blythe could not determine the children's age even with this second clue. However, Alexis's third statement revealed that there was a daughter whose age was greater than the others, so the 3, 4, 4 combination was ruled out.

Inspecting the Troops

59 seconds. The answer is not 58 seconds (twice 29 seconds). Refer to the distance between the first and second troop, or second and third troop, etc., as one segment. There are 29 segments between the first and thirtieth man. The time required was 29 seconds to cover this distance, so the officer rides at the rate of 1 second per segment. There are 59 segments in total, so the total time required will be 59 seconds.

How Many Schlockels?

Altus has 32 schlockels. From clue 1, if the number of schlockels Altus has is a multiple of 5, the number is 5, 10, or 15. However, from clue 2, the number is not 5, 10, or 15, because none of these is a multiple of 8 and none is between 20 and 29. So the number of schlockels Altus has is not a multiple of 5. From this we know that it is also not a multiple of 10—since any number that is a multiple of 10 is a multiple of 5. Hence, from clue 3, Altus has 31, 32, 33, 34, 36, 37, 38, or 39 schlockels. The number cannot be "not a multiple of 8," so it is a multiple of 8. Thus, Altus has 32 schlockels.

Human vs. Minotaur

The human warrior's clockwise counting should begin with the warrior third from the Minotaur, moving clockwise. He numbers the positions 1 to 7 as in the arrangement on the next page, with M, the Minotaur's position, labeled "1." He would then start counting seven places, beginning with "4." This lands him on "3." He defeats "3," then, beginning with "4," he counts clockwise another seven places. This brings him around the circle to "4," with whom he fights the second battle. Continuing in this manner, the order in which the warrior will fight his foes is 3, 4, 6, 2, 5, 7, 1.

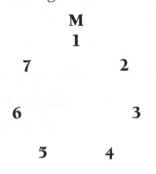

Two Riders

58 miles. In an hour the first rider traveled 30 miles and the second 28 miles, so they were 58 miles apart one hour before they met each other.

Jousting Tournament Number

Sir Bale's number was 5. Four numbers are less than 5: 1, 2, 3, and 4. Six numbers are greater than 5: 6, 7, 8, 9, 10, 11. The product of 4 and 6 is 24. The answer would be the same if Sir Bale's number were 7; then there would be six numbers less than 7 and four numbers greater than 7.

Knights and Their Weapons

C. Only the knight and the weapon next to one another move—the knight up, the weapon down.

Medieval Merry-Go-Round

D. Black and white knights and ladies alternate as they spin counterclockwise. Horse and dragon spin clockwise.

To the King's Castle

8 miles. Alf's answer to Beryl's first question was that the distance from their cottage to the point where she posed the question was three times the distance in miles from that point to the inn. Let x = the distance in miles from that point to the inn.

Alf's answer to Beryl's second question was that the distance to the castle from the point where she asked the second question was three times as far as the distance they had gone since leaving the inn. Let y = the distance in miles they had gone since leaving the inn. The distance between the points on the trip where the two questions were asked was 2 miles. The diagram at right clarifies the puzzle.

Since x + y = 2, it follows that 3(x + y) = 6. But 3 (x + y) is the same as 3x + 3y, distances that are marked in the diagram. The total distance, therefore, is (x + y) + (3x + 3y) miles, which is 2 + 6 = 8 miles.

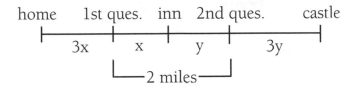

How Many Handshakes?

105. The first knight shakes the hands of fourteen other knights. The second, having already shaken hands with the first, shakes the hands of thirteen others; the third, having shaken hands with the first and second, shakes hands with twelve others, and so forth. So we have the answer: 14 + 13 + 12 + 11 + 10 + 9 + 8 + 7 + 6 + 5 + 4 + 3 + 2 + 1 = 105.

Minotaur Fighters

Logi had 78, Magnus had 42, Nepo had 24. The best way to solve this problem is by making a table that begins at the end of the lending:

Logi		Magnus		Nepo	
48	+	48	+	48	= 144
↓		↓		↓	
24	+	24	+	96	= 144
↓		↓		↓	
12	+	84	+	48	= 144
↓		↓		↓	
72	+	42	+	24	= 144

A Princess or a Dragon? II

The middle cave does not contain a princess, since its sign says it contains a dragon, and the cave containing the princess has a true statement on its sign. Also, if the middle cave contained a dragon, it would not say so, since only the sign on the cave with the princess has a true statement on it. Thus, the middle cave is empty. So, the sign on the middle cave is false. Since the middle cave is empty, the sign on cave C bears a true statement on it. So it contains the princess. The sign above cave A is, by elimination, false, and must contain the dragon.

Genie Hijinks

C. The foods spin counterclockwise around animals.

King Arthur Meets with King Balfour

576 ways. Without loss of generality, choose the knight for seat #2 first. From what we are told, he must be a knight of King Balfour. He can be chosen in four different ways. Next, choose the knight for seat #3. He is a knight of King Arthur, and he too can be chosen in four different ways. Then, seat #4 can be filled in three ways, from among Balfour's remaining three knights. Similarly, seats 7 and 8 can be filled in two ways each, and seats 9 and 10 in two ways each. So the required computation is: $4 \times 4 \times 3 \times 3 \times 2 \times 2 \times 1 \times 1$, which equals 576.

Did the Dragon Catch Pryor?

No, Pryor made it to the sea cave with less than four seconds to spare. If Wivere were to catch up with Pryor, he had to cover 7 miles before Pryor covered 2 miles. Pryor ran at a constant rate of 20 miles per hour, so he covered 2 miles in 6 minutes. As for Wivere, he ran the first mile in 3 minutes, the second in 1.5 minutes, the third in 0.75 minutes, the fourth in 0.375 minutes, the fifth in 0.1875 minutes, the sixth in 0.09375 minutes, and the seventh in 0.046875 minutes. Thus, Wivere needed 5.953125 minutes to run 7 miles. Add to this time the 6 seconds (0.1 minutes) he hesitated, and Wivere reached the sea in 6.053125 minutes, or 6 minutes and about 3.4 seconds.

We can only hope that Pryor wasn't harmed by Wivere's fiery breath!

FANTASTIC PUZZLES

HYPOTHESES

These puzzles contain assumptions that may or may not be valid. To solve them you must differentiate between those that are valid and those that are not valid.

The Voyage of Singood the Sailor

During his growing years, Singood had heard many tales of his illustrious father, Sinbad the Sailor, and the seven voyages during which he was able to amass an enormous fortune. Singood wished to undertake adventures of his own and achieve fabulous wealth, as his father had.

A Giant Fish

Singood signed on as a sailor on a merchant ship. After being at sea for several weeks, the ship was blown far off course by a storm and came within sight of what appeared to be an island. The captain and crew, including Singood, attempted to row ashore.

Amazingly, this happened not to be an island, but the very same giant fish encountered by Singood's father, Sinbad the Sailor, during the first of his seven voyages at sea. The giant predator's method was to give the appearance of an island in order to engulf any and all unsuspecting prey that came near. Singood and his fellow sailors sought to escape by swimming back to the ship.

From the statements below, what time of day was it and what was the outcome of the encounter?

1. If the monster fish had just consumed a merchant ship and several whales and was not interested in another meal, then it was evening.

2. If it was morning, the ship and crew were too small to be noticed by the monster.

3. If it was evening, then the monster fish was too old and slow to catch the ship and crew.

4. If the giant fish was too old and slow to catch the crew and ship, then it was morning.

	too small	too slow	not interested
morning			
evening			

Mark a plus (+) or a minus (−) sign as you determine whether or not a statement is valid.

Solution on page 230.

An Enchanted Island

The ship and crew came within sight of an unknown island. The trees and lovely flowers growing on it convinced them that this time it was really an island.

Singood, the first mate, and the second mate went ashore to explore. Unknown to them, the island was enchanted, and the instant the three set foot on land they fell under a spell and lost their memories. They could recall nothing, not even who they were or why they were there.

From the statements below, which one of A, B, and C was Singood, which one was the first mate, and which one was the second mate?

1. If A was Singood, then B was the first mate.
2. If B was not Singood, then C was the first mate.
3. If A was the first mate, then B was the second mate.

	1st mate	2nd mate	Singood
A			
B			
C			

As in the previous puzzle, mark a plus or minus sign as you draw your conclusions.

Solution on page 231.

A Third Island

Singood decided to take a swim, and the instant he did his memory returned. He called to his shipmates and they were able to return to their ship.

The ship came within sight of another island just as the adventurers were in need of supplies. As they drew near, the sailors beheld a beautiful sight. Wavy palm trees, a glistening waterfall, a crystal clear lake, and many trees laden with ripe fruit could be clearly seen. The captain chose to be cautious and sent Singood, the first mate, and the second mate toward shore in the ship's dinghy.

In spite of Singood's energetic rowing, the island appeared to remain at the same distance as when they had started off. Then, mysteriously, its features began to disappear bit by bit in front of their eyes. Finally, there was nothing left to see but a barren strip of land, which also slowly faded from sight, leaving the sailors with no trace of the land ever having been there.

From the statements that follow, in what order did the principal island features disappear?

1. If the wavy palms vanished first, then the fruit trees vanished third.

2. If the fruit trees vanished third, the waterfall vanished first.

3. If the waterfall vanished first, then the clear lake vanished fourth.

4. If the clear lake vanished fourth, then the fruit trees vanished first.

5. The clear lake vanished first unless either the waterfall or the wavy palms vanished first.

6. If the clear lake vanished first, neither the fruit trees nor the waterfall vanished fourth.

7. If the wavy palms vanished fourth, then the fruit trees did not vanish third.

	1st	2nd	3rd	4th
clear lake				
fruit trees				
waterfall				
wavy palms				

Solution on page 231.

Return to the Ship

When the three sailors turned back toward their ship, they found it was only a distant speck on the horizon. Realizing that Singood was tired from rowing, they decided to take turns at the task of returning to their ship.

From the statements below, what was the order in which they rowed back to the ship?

1. If Singood was not the first to take a turn rowing, then he was the third to take a turn.

2. If the first mate was first to take a turn rowing, then the second mate was second to take a turn.

3. If the second mate was second to take a turn rowing, then the first mate was third to take a turn.

4. If the first mate was third to take a turn rowing, then Singood was second to take a turn.

	1st mate	2nd mate	Singood
1st turn			
2nd turn			
3rd turn			

Solution on page 233.

A Gigantic Bird

The three sailors rowed their boat toward the ship, but before they were even halfway there, a gigantic bird swooped down on them and plucked them up. They were carried to a distant land, where they were deposited in a nest high in a tree.

From the statements that follow, what was the wingspan of the gigantic bird, and how far did it carry the three sailors?

1. If the wingspan of the gigantic bird was either 20 or 30 meters wide, it carried the three sailors for 50 leagues.

2. If the gigantic bird carried the three shipmates 75 leagues, its wingspan was not 40 or 50 meters wide.

3. If the wingspan of the gigantic bird was 40 or 50 meters wide, it carried the three sailors 75 leagues.

4. If the gigantic bird's wingspan was not 40 or 50 meters wide, then it was 20 or 30 meters wide.

	20 or 30m	40 or 50m
50 leagues		
75 leagues		

Solution on page 234.

Attacked by a Giant Serpent

After the gigantic bird deposited Singood, the first mate, and the second mate high in a tree, one of the three scrambled to the ground. He was immediately attacked by a giant serpent.

A second of the three hurried to the rescue, and the two sailors managed to discourage the serpent long enough that they were able to retreat safely back into the tree.

Which one of the three sailors was attacked by the serpent, which one came to the rescue, and which one remained in the tree?

1. If Singood was attacked by the serpent, then the first mate stayed in the tree.

2. If the first mate stayed in the tree, the second mate did not go to the rescue.

3. If the second mate did not stay in the tree, the first mate was attacked by the serpent.

4. If Singood stayed in the tree, the first mate went to the rescue.

	attacked	to rescue	stayed
Singood			
1st mate			
2nd mate			

Solution on page 234.

Captured by the One-Eyed Giant

After the serpent left, the three shipmates began to make their way back to the ship. They hadn't gone far, however, when a storm came up. Seeking refuge in a large cave, they were captured by a manlike creature of enormous size, with only one eye. He deposited them in a corner of the cave, next to a pile of bones. It was apparent that they were to become meals for the giant, if nothing were done.

While the giant slept, blocking the cave entrance with his massive body, the sailors discussed how to escape. Each one had an idea. The three possibilities were: attempt to climb over the giant while he was still sleeping; hide under the pile of bones until the giant left the cave; or sharpen a large stick and stab the giant in the single eye.

From the statements that follow, which shipmate arrived at which idea?

1. If Singood's idea was to stab the giant in the eye, then the second mate's idea was not to hide under the pile of bones.

2. If the first mate's idea was to stab the giant in the eye, or hide under the bones, then Singood's idea was to climb over the sleeping giant.

3. If Singood's idea was to climb over the giant, or to hide under the bones, then the first mate's idea was to stab the giant in the eye.

	climb over	stab giant	under bones
Singood			
1st mate			
2nd mate			

Solution on page 235.

Escape from the Giant

Held captive in the cave by a one-eyed giant, Singood, the first mate, and the second mate considered their options—and did manage to make their escape. The sailors then proceeded on a long journey, which took either two or three months, back to the sea, where they had left their ship.

Which escape idea did they undertake, and how long did the return to the sea take?

1. If the journey took two months, then the three sailors escaped by hiding under a pile of bones.

2. If the journey took three months, then the sailors escaped from the giant by climbing over him while he was asleep.

3. If the sailors escaped from the giant by climbing over him while he was asleep, then the journey took two months.

4. If the sailors did not escape from the giant by stabbing him with a sharpened stick, then the journey took either two or three months.

	climb over	under bones	stab giant
2 months			
3 months			

Solution on page 236.

An Attack by Giant Spiders

At one point during their long trek to the sea, the three sailors suddenly found themselves under attack by three giant spiders that quickly surrounded them. Taking advantage of the many stones lying about, the sailors began throwing them at the spiders. Each sailor singled out a spider and hurled stones with telling accuracy.

Although the spiders were huge and fierce-looking, with long, menacing legs, they were no match for the three sailors, who found the spider legs to be fragile. One spider suffered a damaged and useless leg from one sailor; the second spider suffered two injured and useless legs by a second sailor; and the third spider suffered three damaged and useless legs from the third sailor's attack. The spiders quickly departed.

Which sailor was able to inflict damage to one spider leg, which to two legs, and which to three legs?

1. If the spider with six useful legs was not injured by Singood, then the spider with seven useful legs was injured by Singood.

2. The spider with seven useful legs was injured by the second mate only if the spider with five useful legs was injured by Singood.

3. The spider with six useful legs was not injured by the first mate only if the spider with five useful legs was injured by Singood.

4. The spider with seven useful legs was injured by Singood only if the spider with six useful legs was not injured by the first mate.

	7 legs	6 legs	5 legs
Singood			
1st mate			
2nd mate			

Solution on page 237.

Serpentmares!

Considering the terrifying adventures that Singood was experiencing, it is no wonder that he was having nightmares. One night he dreamed that four giant serpents—a red one, a black one, a yellow one, and a green one—attacked the three sailors, and each was devoured by one of the serpents. No serpent devoured more than one sailor, and the red serpent definitely had a sailor meal.

In the nightmare, which sailor was devoured by which giant serpent?

1. If the second mate was not devoured by either the blue or green serpent, then the first mate was devoured by the red serpent.

2. The second mate was devoured by the blue serpent, unless the first mate was devoured by the red serpent.

3. If Singood was not devoured by either the black serpent or the blue serpent, then the second mate was devoured by the red serpent.

4. If Singood was devoured by the blue serpent, then the first mate was not devoured by the red serpent.

	black	blue	green	red
Singood				
1st mate				
2nd mate				

Solution on page 238.

WHO DUNNIT?

The puzzles in this section involve crimes that have been committed. Your challenge in each puzzle is to determine who is guilty. In each case there are suspects who make statements. To solve each puzzle you must decide who is telling the truth and who is not.

Supermarket Theft

A supermarket theft has occurred. Someone took a fully loaded cart without paying for the groceries. One of three suspects is guilty—but which one? The guilty party's statement is true; the other two are false.

Who is guilty?

A: B took the cart loaded with groceries.

B: A's statement is true.

C: A's statement is false.

A	
B	
C	

Indicate F (False) or T (True) in the boxes as you draw your conclusions.

Solution on page 240.

Bicycle Thefts

Several bicycles have been stolen in town. It is the work of one person, and there are three suspects. Their statements are below. The statement by the guilty party is false; the other two statements are true.

Who is guilty?

A: C did it.

B: A's statement is false.

C: B's statement is true.

A	
B	
C	

Solution on page 241.

Pool Party Push

It was a fun party out by the pool until someone pushed Janie into the water, fully clothed. No one could be quite sure who did it, but the list of suspects was narrowed down to four. Here, they each make one statement. However, only one of the four suspects speaks truthfully. The guilty party can be deduced from their statements.

Who did it?

A: Either B or C did it.

B: I did it.

C: D did it.

D: A did it.

A	
B	
C	
D	

Solution on page 241.

The Impostor Surgeon

An out-of-work medical technician posed as a veterinary surgeon and successfully performed several operations on small animals before he was discovered. However, because he was always seen wearing a surgical mask, his identity was in question.

There are three suspects; one is the impostor. Each suspect makes two statements. The impostor makes one true and one false statement. The veracity of the other two suspects' statements is unknown.

Which one is the impostor?

A: 1. C did it, because he wanted to help animals.
   2. B's first statement is true.

B: 1. I am innocent.
   2. A is the impostor.

C: 1. A's second statement is true.
   2. B's second statement is false.

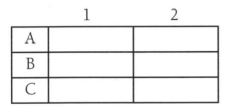

	1	2
A		
B		
C		

Solution on page 242.

Granny Smith's Famous Pecan Pie

Everyone simply raved about Granny Smith's pecan pie! It was famous throughout the county. One day, just before a big Sunday dinner, her famous creation disappeared from the back porch where it had been cooling, never to be seen again.

There were four suspects. Each made a statement, but only one spoke the truth. Their statements follow.

Who did it?

A: I did it.

B: Either A or I did it.

C: D did it.

D: B did it.

A	
B	
C	
D	

Solution on page 242.

Two Scam Hustlers

Two hustlers were working a scam together. They were attempting to convince elderly people that they could double their money if they would give them their Social Security checks.

Five suspects have been identified. Each one makes a statement. The two guilty suspects make false statements. The other three make true statements.

Which two are guilty?

A: E is not one of the guilty parties.

B: C is not guilty.

C: D is innocent.

D: If B is not guilty, then A is guilty.

E: C is guilty.

A	
B	
C	
D	
E	

Solution on page 243.

Who Stole the Goat?

Two semi-pro football teams are arch rivals. A member of the Lions stole the mascot of the rival team, the Goats, the night before the big game and didn't return it until the day after the game. There are four suspects: the quarterback, the center, the running back, and the defensive end. Each makes two statements.

The statements by the quarterback and the center are false; the running back makes one true and one false statement, and the defensive end makes two true statements.

From their statements below, which one is which suspect, and who did it?

A: 1. I am not the running back.
   2. The center did it.

B: 1. I am not the quarterback.
   2. The running back did it.

C: 1. I am not the center.
   2. The defensive end did it.

D: 1. I am not the defensive end.
   2. The quarterback did it.

	1	2	football position
A			
B			
C			
D			

Solution on page 244.

What's the Crime?

A crime has been committed. The police are not sure what it is, but there are three suspects and they all have bad reputations. They make the statements below. Each makes one true and two false statements. What was the crime and which suspect did it?

A: 1. I stole a car.
  2. B is innocent.
  3. C is a disreputable person.

B: 1. I robbed a service station.
  2. I stole a car.
  3. A is guilty.

C: 1. I robbed a service station.
  2. B's first statement is false.
  3. A is innocent.

	1	2	3
A			
B			
C			

Solution on page 245.

The Hood-Ornament Thefts

A thief was stealing Mercedes-Benz hood ornaments and selling them for use as necklaces. The sheriff interrogated four suspects who had been seen hanging around the Mercedes-Benz dealership. Their statements are below.

Little is known as to the suspects' truthfulness except that only one of the guilty party's statements is true.

A. 1. I wouldn't recognize a Mercedes Benz if I saw one.
   2. B didn't do it.

B. 1. A's second statement is true.
   2. A did it.

C. 1. A would certainly recognize a Mercedes Benz if he saw one.
   2. At least one of B's statements is true.

D. 1. Both of B's statements are false.
   2. I wouldn't recognize a Mercedes Benz if I saw one.

	1	2
A		
B		
C		
D		

Solution on page 245.

Thanksgiving Dinner

Mrs. Olsen had spent all day preparing for a festive Thanksgiving family dinner. The family was enjoying refreshments in the living room before dinner. The cooked turkey, which had been set near the kitchen door in readiness for the feast, disappeared—taken by a thief who had apparently smelled the mouthwatering turkey aroma through an open window.

Three suspects were identified, and one of them is guilty. Their statements follow. Each suspect makes at least one false statement.

Who stole the turkey?

A: 1. Either B or I did it.
   2. I agree with B's second statement.

B: 1. I agree with A's first statement.
   2. C is innocent.

C: 1. I agree with A's second statement.
   2. A did it and B helped him.

	1	2
A		
B		
C		

Solution on page 246.

Car Thefts

In a southern Arizona town, several Ford Mustangs have been stolen, apparently to be sold in Mexico. Three suspects, known thieves, have been identified. One of them is guilty.

One suspect makes three true statements, and one makes three false statements. How the third suspect responds is unknown. Which one stole the Mustangs?

A: 1. I am innocent.
2. All of my statements are untruthful.
3. I am opposed to all crime, especially car thefts.

B: 1. I did not do it.
2. Only one of my statements is untruthful.
3. I am opposed to all crime, especially car thefts.

C: 1. I did not do it.
2. I always speak truthfully.
3. I understand that Ford Mustangs are popular in Mexico.

	1	2	3
A			
B			
C			

Solution on page 246.

Residential Burglaries

A series of residential burglaries caused concern in the neighborhood. The police inspector concentrated on solving these crimes and has come up with three suspects. One of them is guilty.

The suspects make the following statements. Each suspect makes at least two false statements.

Who is the burglar?

A: 1. B and C are strangers to each other.
    2. I am the burglar.
    3. B's second statement is not truthful.

B: 1. I don't know C.
    2. C is the burglar.
    3. A's third statement is false.

C: 1. A is the burglar.
   2. I am acquainted with B.
   3. If I had wanted to be a burglar, I would have picked a more affluent neighborhood.

	1	2	3
A			
B			
C			

Solution on page 247.

Who Cheated at Poker?

Five poker players were enjoying a game when, during one hand, five aces turned up. Clearly, someone had cheated.

The players' statements follow. Each makes one true and one false statement. Who cheated?

A: 1. I am certainly innocent.
   2. I have no idea who cheated.

B: 1. C is innocent.
   2. Neither A nor D cheated.

C: 1. B's first statement is true.

    2. B was the cheater.

D: 1. B did it.

    2. B's second statement is true.

E: 1. A was one of the players that day.

    2. D's second statement is false.

	1	2
A		
B		
C		
D		
E		

Solution on page 248.

Which of the Three Is Innocent?

Two crimes have been committed in the Williamson family. The culprits are two of the family's three boys. However, all three confess. Perhaps the third boy did not want to be different.

At any rate, the two culprits truthfully admit their crimes and the third boy falsely confesses to a crime. Each boy makes one true and two false statements.

Which boy is innocent?

Junior
1. Timmy's first statement is false.
2. Sonny's first statement is true.
3. I took some money from the dresser.

Sonny
1. I played hooky from school today.
2. Timmy's first statement is false.
3. Junior's third statement is false.

Timmy
1. I kicked the dog.
2. Sonny's first statement is true.
3. Junior's third statement is false.

	1	2	3
Junior			
Sonny			
Timmy			

Solution on page 249.

Who Put the Rattlesnake in Henry's Garage?

"I suppose it was just a prank," Henry said. The fact, though, is that rattlesnakes are quite dangerous and somebody did put a live one in Henry's garage.

There are three suspects. Their statements are true, except for any directly mentioning the culprit. Which one is guilty?

A: 1. C is not guilty.

   2. Rattlesnakes are not good for you.

B: 1. A's first statement is false.

   2. C's first statement is true.

C: 1. I wouldn't go near a rattlesnake.

   2. A is not guilty.

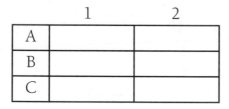

	1	2
A		
B		
C		

Solution on page 250.

Stolen Golf Clubs

At the Mountain Golf Club, a set of expensive left-handed golf clubs has been stolen. The evidence points to three of the club's employees who were on duty during the time that the golf clubs were taken and who are known to be left-handed golfers. One of these employees did it.

Each makes three statements, although no two suspects make the same number of true statements. Which suspect is guilty?

A: 1. C is left-handed.
2. B's statements are all false.
3. I don't play golf.

B: 1. A's first statement is true.
2. C's first statement is true.
3. A took the golf clubs.

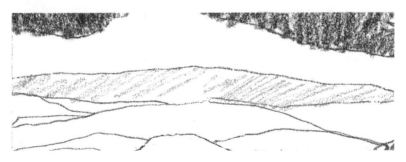

C: 1. B is not guilty.
   2. B was on duty during the time of the theft.
   3. I am not left-handed.

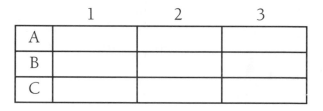

	1	2	3
A			
B			
C			

Solution on page 250.

Who Stole the Baseball Mitt?

A famous baseball player was in the city to play in a game. Just before it was to begin, the discovery was made that the player's favorite mitt had been stolen. The police were able to identify and question three suspects, who had been seen hanging around the clubhouse and were known to sell stolen property. One of them stole the mitt.

Each suspect makes the same number of true and false statements. Which one is the thief?

A: 1. I have a record of committing this type of crime.
   2. C did it.
   3. B does not need it, so he would not have stolen it.

B: 1. I don't need it, so I would not have stolen it.

2. I'm sure neither C nor I would commit a crime.

3. A has a record of committing this type of crime.

C: 1. A is not a likely suspect.

2. B did it.

3. B's first statement is false.

	1	2	3
A			
B			
C			

Solution on page 251.

Who Stole Golf Cart No. 22?

One Halloween night, four revelers were having a great time being mischievous in the vicinity of the Mountain Golf Club, when their fun got out of hand. One of the four, in the presence of the other three, stole a golf cart and proceeded to drive it over several of the greens, damaging them.

The next day, the four revelers were questioned, and only one of them made no false statements.

Which one stole the cart and damaged the greens?

A: 1. I wasn't there.

   2. B was looking for trouble; she did it.

   3. When I arrived, the damage was done.

B: 1. I was there.

   2. C stole the cart.

   3. A is innocent; he tried to stop it.

C: 1. A's first statement is true.

   2. D did it.

   3. A's third statement is false.

D: 1. C's third statement is false.

   2. A's first statement is false.

   3. Neither B nor I did it.

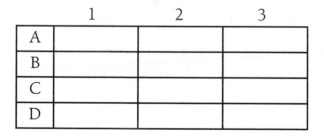

	1	2	3
A			
B			
C			
D			

Solution on page 252.

Unsavory Characters

A load of Christmas toys that had just arrived at the local toy store was stolen. Four individuals who had unsavory reputations were questioned by the police. Each had been seen in the area, and all four knew who stole the toys.

The guilty party made one true and two false statements. The truthfulness of the statements by the other suspects is unknown.

A: 1. I was out of town when the theft occurred.

    2. D is guilty.

    3. I think the toys were just lost.

B: 1. A lied when he said he was out of town.

    2. C is innocent.

    3. I do not understand why I am a suspect.

C: 1. A lied when he said he was out of town when the theft occurred.

    2. I am innocent.

    3. I'll bet A knows who did it.

D: 1. I understand why I am suspect.

    2. C is guilty.

    3. I am innocent.

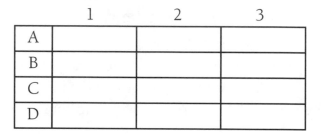

	1	2	3
A			
B			
C			
D			

Solution on page 253.

Who Is the Shoplifter?

There has been a series of shoplifting thefts from stores in the town mall. Thanks to careful observations on the part of employees in several stores, three suspects have been identified, and it is clear that one of them is guilty.

Their statements follow. However, the culprit makes three false statements; one of the other two suspects makes two true statements and one false statement; and one makes one true and two false statements.

Which one is the shoplifter?

A: 1. C's first statement is false.
2. C did it.
3. I am not the most likely suspect.

B: 1. A is the most likely suspect.
   2. I only heard about the thefts later.
   3. I am innocent.

C: 1. B's first statement is not true.
   2. A did it.
   3. B's second statement is false.

	1	2	3
A			
B			
C			

Solution on page 253.

LETTERS FOR DIGITS

In the addition and subtraction problems in this section, digits have been replaced by letters. In these puzzles, each letter represents the same digit wherever it occurs in the given puzzle.

Subtraction, Three Digits

Each digit has been replaced by a letter. Each letter represents the same digit wherever it occurs. The digits are 0, 4, and 8.

```
   A  C  A
 - C  C  C
 ─────────
   C  B  C
```

Determine the digit represented by each letter.

Solution on page 255.

Addition, Four Digits

Each digit has been replaced by a letter. Each letter represents the same digit wherever it occurs. The digits are 1, 2, 3, and 4.

```
   A  A
 + B  C
 ───────
   C  D
```

Identify the digit represented by each letter.

Solution on page 256.

Subtraction, Four Digits

Each letter represents the same digit wherever it occurs in the puzzle. The digits are 2, 4, 6, and 8.

```
   A  B  C
 - B  D  B
 ─────────
   D  D  B
```

What digit is represented by each letter?

Solution on page 257.

Addition, Five Digits

Each letter in this addition problem represents the same digit wherever it occurs. The digits are 1, 2, 3, 4, and 5.

```
   A  A  E
 + E  A  C
 ─────────
   B  D  D
```

Determine the digit represented by each letter.

Solution on page 258.

Addition, Six Digits

Each letter in this addition problem represents the same digit wherever it occurs. The digits are 0, 2, 3, 4, 5, and 6.

```
  A E A C A
+ E E A B D
---------
  F C D C C
```

What digit is represented by each letter?

Solution on page 259.

Addition, Six Digits Again

Each letter stands for the same digit wherever it occurs. The digits are 0, 1, 3, 5, 7, and 9.

```
  B C E C
+ E C E F
---------
A E E A D
```

What does each letter stand for?

Solution on page 260.

Subtraction, Five Digits

Each letter represents a digit wherever it occurs in the puzzle. The digits are 2, 3, 5, 7, and 9.

```
  A  C  E
- C  E  D
---------
  F  F  F
```

Determine the digit represented by each letter.

Solution on page 261.

Addition, Eight Digits

Each letter has been substituted for one of the eight digits. The digits are 0, 1, 2, 3, 4, 5, 6, and 7.

```
  C  D  A  F  C
+ C  D  C  B  H
--------------
H E  C  E  G  F
```

What digit is represented by each letter?

Solution on page 262.

Addition, Eight Digits Again

Each letter stands for the same digit wherever it occurs. The digits are 2, 3, 4, 5, 6, 7, 8, and 9.

```
      B C
  E E F E C
  E H D H A
+ H E A E H
─────────────
  F G G B H
```

Determine the digit represented by each letter.

Solution on page 263.

Addition, Seven Digits

Each letter represents the same digit wherever it occurs. The digits are 1, 2, 3, 4, 5, 7, and 8.

```
  G D B E G A
  D D F B A A
+ D G C B A A
─────────────
A E G A B C G
```

What does each letter stand for?

Solution on page 265.

DESERT FOOTHILLS GOLF

A nine-hole desert golf course was designed by a highly regarded but very eccentric genius who went overboard in designing it. The course is reportedly very challenging. However, the challenge is not so much the difficulty of the golf course as it is of finding your way from each green to the next tee. It seems there's the matter of mountain lions, rattlesnakes, gila monsters, scorpions, and spiny cactus at virtually every step away from the fairways and greens, in addition to the desert heat and lack of water, so many an unaware golfer has met with severe misfortune.

The First Decision

A lone vacationing golfer happens upon a sign advertising challenging desert foothills golf, and he accepts the challenge. There appears to be nothing especially challenging about the first hole. The fairway is straight and flat, and there appear to be no obstacles; he is a little disappointed.

The situation changes when he leaves the green and looks for the second tee. No tee is within sight. What he finds are two paths with a sign posted at each. In reading the scorecard, he finds a reference to paths that lead the golfer from each green to the next tee. It states:

"Directional signs indicate the correct paths."

In small print, a notation states that at least one of the signs to the second tee is false. He inspects the two signs.

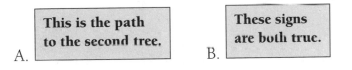

A.
This is the path to the second tree.

B.
These signs are both true.

Which path should be taken?

	sign A	sign B
If path A		
If path B		

Assume each path in turn is the path to take. Indicate T (for True) or F (for False) near sign A and sign B in each case.

Solution on page 267.

The Second Decision

The golfer manages to select the correct path, and before long he is playing the second hole. This time, on leaving the green, he sees not two but three paths, one of which is purported to lead to the third tee. Three signs, one at each path, are his clues.

He again consults his scorecard and reads that the correct decision could conclusively be made. The path signs are below:

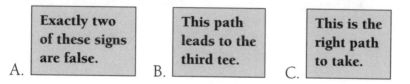

A. **Exactly two of these signs are false.**

B. **This path leads to the third tee.**

C. **This is the right path to take.**

Which path should the golfer select?

	sign A	sign B	sign C
If path A			
If path B			
If path C			

Solution on page 268.

The Third Decision

Again, he makes the right decision, but so far the golf course doesn't seem very appealing. He plays the third hole and, as anticipated, encounters three more paths with accompanying signs. His scorecard, in barely legible print, states that only one of the three signs is true. He reads the signs, as follows:

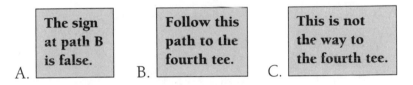

A. **The sign at path B is false.**

B. **Follow this path to the fourth tee.**

C. **This is not the way to the fourth tee.**

Which path should be taken?

	sign A	sign B	sign C
If path A			
If path B			
If path C			

Solution on page 268.

The Fourth Decision

After arriving safely at the fourth tee and playing the hole, the golfer prepares himself for what he knows will be another challenge that is not nearly as much fun as golf. He sees three more paths, with a sign next to each, and only one leads to the fifth tee. His scorecard says that at least one sign is false. He reads the signs as follows:

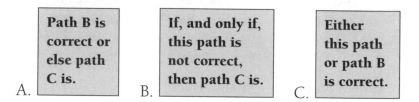

A. **Path B is correct or else path C is.**

B. **If, and only if, this path is not correct, then path C is.**

C. **Either this path or path B is correct.**

Which is the correct path?

	sign A	sign B	sign C
If path A			
If path B			
If path C			

Solution on page 269.

The Fifth Decision

The fifth hole isn't much fun, since he is thinking too much about the next set of signs. After completing the fifth hole, he is confronted by three more paths and their signs. According to the fine print in his score-card, exactly one of the signs is false. He reads them as follows:

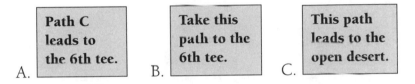

A. **Path C leads to the 6th tee.**
B. **Take this path to the 6th tee.**
C. **This path leads to the open desert.**

Which path should the golfer take?

	sign A	sign B	sign C
If path A			
If path B			
If path C			

Solution on page 270.

The Sixth Decision

Once again the golfer's reasoning is correct. Those beads of perspiration aren't from the heat, though. He plays the sixth hole without much enthusiasm, and approaches the next set of paths, hoping to get safely to the seventh tee.

His scorecard says that exactly one of the signs is false. He reads the signs, below:

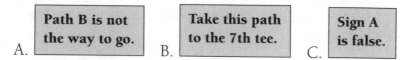

A. **Path B is not the way to go.**

B. **Take this path to the 7th tee.**

C. **Sign A is false.**

Which path should be taken?

	sign A	sign B	sign C
If path A			
If path B			
If path C			

Solution on page 271.

The Seventh Decision

The golfer has made several correct decisions and is
gaining in confidence. Perhaps now he can manage to
concentrate on his golf game. He plays well at the
seventh hole, and approaches the next set of signs
without quite as much nervousness. He consults his
scorecard, which indicates that the sign at the path to
take is the only false sign. His confidence evaporates.
The signs are as follows:

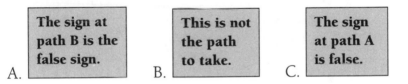

A. **The sign at path B is the false sign.**

B. **This is not the path to take.**

C. **The sign at path A is false.**

Which path is the correct one?

	sign A	sign B	sign C
If path A			
If path B			
If path C			

Solution on page 272.

The Eighth Decision

He has made seven correct decisions in a row and is finding it difficult to focus on his golf swing. However, he must face his next challenge, and it comes after a double bogey on the eighth hole. The golfer's scorecard tells him that one false sign points the way to the ninth tee, but the other two signs lead to open desert. He reads them as follows:

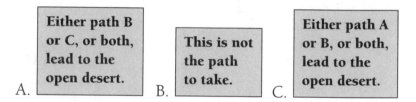

A. **Either path B or C, or both, lead to the open desert.**

B. **This is not the path to take.**

C. **Either path A or B, or both, lead to the open desert.**

Which path is correct?

	sign A	sign B	sign C
If path A			
If path B			
If path C			

Solution on page 273.

The Ninth Decision

The golfer finishes the ninth hole with another double bogey. It is a long way back to the clubhouse, and it is getting late. He quickly moves to the paths that await him. His scorecard indicates that at least two signs are false. He reads them carefully, below:

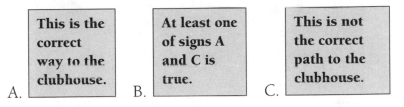

A. **This is the correct way to the clubhouse.**

B. **At least one of signs A and C is true.**

C. **This is not the correct path to the clubhouse.**

It has been dark for several hours, and the golfer hasn't returned to the clubhouse. He apparently took the wrong path. Which one should he have taken?

	sign A	sign B	sign C
If path A			
If path B			
If path C			

Solution on page 274.

NAMESAKES

These puzzles involve the names of people and of other things. Your challenge is to correctly connect people's names with other names: who's named for what, and what's named for whom.

Four Fishing Boats

Four close friends who are avid fishermen as well as horse owners have each named his fishing boat after the horse owned by one of the others. No two boats have the same name.

From the statements that follow, what is the name of each horse (one is Spike) and what name is given to each boat?

1. Jake's fishing boat is named after Jay's horse.

2. Jeb's horse is named King.

3. Joe's fishing boat is named Ace.

4. Jeb's fishing boat is not named Beau.

	horse	boat
Jake		
Jay		
Jeb		
Joe		

Solution on page 275.

Knowheyan Paddle-Bird Tournament

Knowhey is a planet in another galaxy on which a favorite game of the inhabitants is played with two or four players and involves hitting a feathered ball back and forth over a net, using paddles. The inhabitants are very adept at this game, and enjoy playing with visitors from other planets. An informal tournament is being played in which four teams are participating; each is comprised of one visitor and one inhabitant. Because the inhabitants' names are difficult to pronounce, to be congenial each Knowheyan player has adopted the name of one of the visitors, although no inhabitant is the namesake of the visitor with which he is teamed and no two teams contain the same pair of names.

From the following statements, determine which visitor is teamed with which inhabitant.

1. The visitor Larry is teamed with the inhabitant who is the namesake of the visitor who is teamed with the inhabitant using the name Lenny.

2. The visitor Lenny is teamed with the inhabitant who is the namesake of the visitor who is teamed with the inhabitant Larry.

3. The visitor Logan is teamed with the inhabitant who is the namesake of the visitor who is teamed with the inhabitant Lewis.

4. The inhabitant Lenny and his teammate won their game with the visitor Logan and his teammate.

	Larry	Lenny	Logan	Lewis
Larry				
Lenny				
Logan				
Lewis				

Solution on page 276.

Burglaries in the Neighborhood

There has been a series of neighborhood burglaries, and six neighbors have acquired six dogs, ostensibly to serve as watchdogs. For some reason, the six neighbors each named his dog after one of the other neighbors, yet no two dogs were named after the same neighbor. (One of the six neighbors, it turns out, is the burglar.)

Based on the statements that follow, which neighbor owns which dog, and who is the burglar?

1. The dog named Moriarity is owned by the owner whose namesake is owned by Milton.

2. The dog named Marion is owned by the owner whose namesake is owned by Melville.

3. Milton's dog is not named Maurice or Martin.

4. The dog named Martin is owned by the owner whose namesake is owned by the owner whose namesake is owned by the burglar.

5. The dog named Melville is owned by the owner whose namesake is owned by Martin.

6. Milton's dog is the namesake of the owner of the dog whose namesake is the owner of the dog named Marion.

Dogs

Owners	Marion	Martin	Maurice	Melville	Milton	Moriarity
Marion						
Martin						
Maurice						
Melville						
Milton						
Moriarity						

Solution on page 277.

THINGS IN ORDER

These puzzles involve putting things (and people) in order. The reasoning process used in solving the following puzzles is unlike that used for the other puzzles in the book. No diagrams are needed, nor are any assumptions or considerations of veracity required. The challenge is to take the items listed and arrange them in the proper order, as described.

To solve these puzzles, list the items generally in the order described. Then carefully review the information given, and adjust the order of the items listed until it is completely consistent with the information provided. For most puzzles, this will require several realignments.

Wood-Chopping Contest

In late autumn, the forest dwellers known as the Forest People held their annual wood-chopping contest to provide fuel to last through the winter. Each participant was then ranked according to the amount of wood he chopped. On this particular occasion, twelve of these forest denizens competed. From the following information, list the twelve participants in order, according to the amount of wood each chopped.

Evum chopped more wood than Estum, Edum, Eskum, and Ensum, and less than Egum, Elfum, Efrum, and Ekum. Ekum chopped less than Epum, and more than Esum, Eskum, and Ebum. Egum chopped more wood than Epum, who chopped more than Elfum, Estum, and Evum.

Eskum chopped more than Ensum, who chopped less than Esum, Evum, and Ebum. Ebum chopped less than Estum and Edum. Edum chopped less than Esum. Elfum chopped more than Efrum, who chopped more than Ekum and Evum. Evum chopped more than Esum, who chopped less than Estum, who chopped more than Ebum, who chopped more than Eskum and less than Edum.

Solution on page 278.

Trees in the Forest

Many different varieties of tree grow in the forest inhabited by the Forest People. Walking along a small path, Ekum counted eighteen varieties of tree. Based on the statements that follow, in what order were the different varieties of tree aligned on each side of the path? ("Before and after" refers to the same side of the path. "Across from" means directly opposite, on the other side of the path.)

A cedar, which was after a birch, was before an elm, a fir, and an oak, which was across from a poplar, which was after an ash, a yew, and an aspen. A hickory was across from a maple, which was after the oak and the elm, which was after a willow. A pine was before the birch, which was after a hemlock, which was before the fir and across from an alder, which was after the aspen and before a juniper and a spruce, which was before the yew. A tamarack was before the poplar, which was before the hickory. The juniper was before the spruce, which was before the tamarack, which was before the ash and after the yew. The fir was before the willow and across from the yew.

Solution on page 278.

Fishing Flies

Henry Hackle is the proprietor of the Midville Fly-Fishing Shop. Part of his job is answering inquiries from his customers. Henry has been asked what his favorite fishing flies are and how he rates them, one to another. He has managed to narrow the list to sixteen, but has difficulty rating them in order of preference. The best he can do is compare each favorite fly to a few others.

You can help out by listing all of his favorite flies in the order in which they are favored, based on the information below:

The Gold-Ribbed Hare's Ear is favored ahead of the Woolly Bugger, the Grey Wulff, and the Zug Bug, but behind the Olive Blue Dun and the Adams. The Royal Wulff, the Wright's Royal, and the Royal Humpy are favored ahead of the Light Cahill, the Elk-Hair Caddis, and the Brook's Stone Fly, but behind the Maribou Muddler, which is favored ahead of the Grey Wulff and the Prince Nymph. Murphy's No. 1 is favored ahead of the Adams, the Elk-Hair Caddis, the Gold-Ribbed Hare's Ear, and the Woolly Bugger, which is favored ahead of the Maribou Muddler and the Joe's Hopper, which is rated behind the Zug Bug.

The Grey Wulff is favored ahead of the Elk-hair Caddis, the Royal Humpy, and the Light Cahill, but behind the Royal Wulff, the Olive Blue Dun, and the Adams. The Royal Wulff is favored behind the Woolly Bugger and Murphy's No. 1, but ahead of the Wright's Royal, which is less favored than the Royal Humpy. The Prince Nymph is favored ahead of the Zug Bug and the Brook's Stone Fly, which is favored ahead of the Zug Bug.

The Olive Blue Dun is favored ahead of the Maribou Muddler and the Gold-Ribbed Hare's Ear, but behind the Adams. The Elk-Hair Caddis is favored behind the Wright's Royal and the Maribou Muddler, but ahead of the Light Cahill, which is favored ahead of the Joe's Hopper and the Prince Nymph.

Solution on page 279.

Varieties of Fruit

The ideal climate in the land of Hyperborea provided for the availability of a wide variety of fruit. At the fresh fruit stand in one village market, twenty varieties could be found arranged in two rows. Based on the information that follows, list the varieties of fruit in their proper order. ("To the right of" and "to the left of" mean in the same row; "in front of" or "behind" means directly opposite in the adjacent row.)

The grapes were to the right of the lemons and the mangos, which were to the left of the nectarines, which were in front of the papayas. The cherries, which were behind the strawberries and to the right of the plums, were to the left of the persimmons, which were to the right of the loquats, which were to the left of the apricots. The oranges were to the right of the pears and to the left of the plums, which were to the right of the peaches, which were to the left of the cherries and to the right of the oranges.

The limes, which were in front of the pears, were to the left of the watermelons and the bananas, which were to the left of the blackberries, which were to the right of the watermelons, which were to the left of the strawberries and the bananas. The raspberries were to the left of the lemons, which were to the right of the blackberries and the strawberries, which were to the right of the bananas and to the left of the raspberries and the mangos, which were to the right of the lemons.

The nectarines were to the left of the grapes, which were to the right of the raspberries, which were to the right of the strawberries. The papayas were to the left of the guavas, which were to the right of the loquats, which were to the right of the cherries and to the left of the persimmons, which were to the left of the apricots.

Solution on page 279.

New Neighbors

Twenty-four families have recently moved into town on one new street. From the information presented below, can you determine the relative location of the home of each family on the street? ("To the right of" or "to the left of" means on the same side of the street. "Across from" means on the other side of the street and directly opposite, facing into the street.)

The Maloneys' house is to the left of the Mayers, the Mayfields, and the Marlows, and across the street from the Mahoneys, who live on the east side of the street. The Mallettes live to the left of the Marlows, the Mastersons, and the Mallorys, who live to the right of the Malones, the Maxwells, and the Mayers. The Matlocks live to the right of the Mayfields, who live to the right of the Marshes and the Mallorys.

The Mathesons live to the right of the Marleaus, the Martins, and the Marquardts, who live to the right of the Macklins and the Matsens.

The Marshalls live to the left of the Mahoneys and to the right of the Mathesons, the Marleaus, and the Martins. The Mathews live to the left of the Majors and the Marquardts, and to the right of the Matsens, who live to the right of the Macklins.

The Malones live to the left of the Mastersons, who live to the left of the Mallorys and to the right of the Mayburys, who live to the left of the Malones and to the right of the Marlows. The Majors live to the left of the Martins and to the right of the Magnans, who live to the right of the Marquardts, who live to the right of the Marsdens.

The Marleaus live to the left of the Mathesons and to the right of the Martins. The Mallettes live to the left of the Marlows and to the right of the Maxwells, who live to the right of the Mayers. The Marshes live to the right of the Mallorys.

Solution on page 280.

SOLUTIONS

HYPOTHESES:
The Voyage of Singood the Sailor

A Giant Fish

CONSIDERATIONS

From statement 1, if the fish had just consumed a ship and several whales, it was evening. From statement 3, if it was evening, the giant fish was too old and slow. Therefore, statement 1 is not valid: the giant fish had not just consumed a ship and several whales.

From statement 4, if the giant fish was too old, it was morning. From statement 2, if it was morning, the ship and crew were too small to be noticed. Therefore, statement 4 is not valid: the giant fish was not too old and slow.

Therefore, the solution must be that it was morning and the ship and crew were too small to be noticed by the giant fish.

SUMMARY SOLUTION

It was morning, and the ship and crew were too small to be noticed by the giant fish.

An Enchanted Island

CONSIDERATIONS

From statement 3, if A was the first mate, B was the second mate. However, from statement 2, if B was not Singood, then C was the first mate. Therefore, we can conclude that A was not the first mate and, from statement 2, B was not the first mate. Therefore, C was the first mate.

From statement 1, since B was not the first mate, A was not Singood. Therefore, A was the second mate and B was Singood. (Note: Even though the "if" part of statement 2 is invalid [B was Singood], this does not preclude C's being the first mate.)

SUMMARY SOLUTION

A was the second mate.

B was Singood.

C was the first mate.

A Third Island

CONSIDERATIONS

From statement 1, if the palms vanished first, the fruit trees were third. However, from statement 2, if the fruit trees were third to vanish, the waterfall was first. Therefore, the palms did not vanish first.

From statement 3, if the waterfall vanished first, the clear lake vanished fourth. However, from statement 4, if the clear lake was fourth, the fruit trees were first. Therefore, the waterfall was not first.

From statement 5, since neither the waterfall nor the wavy palms vanished first, the clear lake vanished first.

From statement 6, since the clear lake vanished first, the fruit trees and waterfall must have vanished second and third in some order, and the wavy palms vanished fourth.

From statement 7, since the wavy palms vanished fourth, the waterfall vanished third and the fruit trees vanished second.

SUMMARY SOLUTION

clear lake	1st
fruit trees	2nd
waterfall	3rd
wavy palms	4th

Return to the Ship

CONSIDERATIONS

From statement 1, we can conclude that Singood was either first or third to take a turn rowing.

From statement 2, if the first mate was first to take a turn rowing, the second mate was second to take a turn. However, from statement 3, if the second mate was second to take a turn, the first mate was third in the rotation. Therefore, the assumption in statement 2, that the first mate was first to take a turn, is not valid. The first mate was either second or third in the rowing rotation.

From statement 4, for the first mate to be third to take a turn, Singood must be second to take a turn. However, from statement 1, we know that Singood was either first or third to take a turn. Therefore, the first mate was not third. Therefore, he was second to take a turn.

From statement 5, since the second mate was not second to take a turn, the assumption that he was not third is invalid. The second mate was third and Singood was first in the rotation.

SUMMARY SOLUTION

Singood   1st
first mate   2nd
second mate   3rd

A Gigantic Bird

CONSIDERATIONS

From statements 2 and 3, statement 3 is invalid: the gigantic bird's wingspan was not 40 or 50 meters wide.

From statement 4, the gigantic bird's wingspan was 20 or 30 meters wide.

Therefore, from statement 1, it carried the three shipmates 50 leagues.

SUMMARY SOLUTION

Bird's wingspan was 20 or 30 meters wide; it carried the shipmates 50 leagues.

Attacked by a Giant Serpent

CONSIDERATIONS

From statement 1, if Singood was attacked by the serpent, the first mate stayed in the tree. If so, the second mate must have hurried to the rescue. From statement 2, if the first mate stayed in the tree, the second mate did not go to the rescue. Therefore, Singood was not attacked by the serpent.

From statement 3, if the second mate did not stay in the tree, the first mate was attacked by the serpent. Therefore, the second mate was not attacked by the serpent. Therefore, the first mate was attacked by the serpent.

From statement 4, if Singood stayed in the tree, the first mate went to the rescue. Therefore, Singood did not stay in the tree. Therefore, Singood went to the rescue, and the second mate stayed in the tree.

SUMMARY SOLUTION

Singood — went to rescue
first mate — attacked by serpent
second mate — stayed in tree

Captured by the One-Eyed Giant

CONSIDERATIONS

If statement 1 is valid, then Singood's idea was to stab the giant in his one eye, the second mate's idea was to climb over the sleeping giant, and the first mate's idea was to hide under the bones. From statement 2, if the first mate's idea was to stab the giant in the eye or hide under the bones, then Singood's idea was to climb over the giant. Therefore, we can conclude that statement 1 is not valid: Singood's idea was not to stab the giant in the eye.

From statement 3, if Singood's idea was either of the other two options, then the first mate's idea was to stab the giant in the eye. Therefore, the first mate's idea was to stab the giant. From statement 2, Singood's idea was to climb over the sleeping giant, and the second mate's idea was to hide under the pile of bones.

SUMMARY SOLUTION

Singood — climb over sleeping giant

first mate — stab giant in eye

second mate — hide under bones

Escape from the Giant

CONSIDERATIONS

From statement 2, if the journey took three months, the escape was by climbing over the sleeping giant. From statement 3, the journey took two months if the escape was by climbing over the sleeping giant. There-fore, the journey did not take three months; it took two months.

Statement 3 is invalid, since the escape by climbing over the sleeping giant depended on the journey's taking two months. However, from statement 1, if the journey took two months, then the escape was by hiding beneath a pile of bones.

Statement 4 is valid; the escape was not by stabbing the giant in the eye, since the journey took two months.

Therefore, the escape was by hiding beneath a pile of bones until the giant left the cave, and the journey took two months.

SUMMARY SOLUTION

Escape made by hiding under bones; journey took two months.

An Attack by Giant Spiders

CONSIDERATIONS

From statement 1, since either the spider with six useful legs or the spider with seven useful legs was injured by Singood, the spider with five legs was not injured by Singood.

From statement 2, since the spider with five useful legs was not injured by Singood, the spider with seven useful legs was not injured by the second mate.

From statement 3, since the spider with five useful legs was not injured by Singood, the spider with six useful legs was not injured by the first mate. Therefore, by statement 4, the spider with seven useful legs was injured by Singood.

Therefore, it's the spider with six useful legs that was injured by the second mate, and the spider with five useful legs was injured by the first mate.

SUMMARY SOLUTION

Singood—spider with 7 useful legs
first mate—spider with 5 useful legs
second mate—spider with 6 useful legs

Serpentmares!

CONSIDERATIONS

From statement 3, if Singood was not devoured by either the black or blue serpent, the second mate was devoured by the red serpent. Therefore, Singood was not devoured by the red serpent.

From statement 1, if the second mate was not eaten by either the blue serpent or the green serpent, the first mate was devoured by the red serpent. Therefore, the second mate was not devoured by the red serpent; the first mate was devoured by the red serpent.

Therefore, according to statement 4, Singood was not devoured by the blue serpent. Therefore, since, from statement 3, the second mate was not devoured by the red serpent, Singood had to be devoured by the black serpent.

From statement 2, the second mate was devoured by the green serpent. The blue serpent went away hungry.

SUMMARY SOLUTION
Singood — black serpent
first mate — red serpent
second mate — green serpent

WHO DUNNIT?

Supermarket Theft

CONSIDERATIONS

Consider that the guilty party's statement is true; the other two statements are false.

Assume that A is guilty. If so, A's statement must be true, making B guilty. Therefore, A is not the thief.

Assume B did it. However, since there is only one true statement, B's statement, that A's statement is true, makes two true statements. Therefore, B is innocent. Therefore, C's statement that A's statement is false is true. C is guilty.

SUMMARY SOLUTION

C is the thief.

Bicycle Thefts

CONSIDERATIONS

Consider that the statement by the guilty party is false and the other statements are true.

Assume that B is guilty. If so, B's statement must be false, and A's statement must be true, making C guilty. Therefore, since only one is guilty, it is not B. Assume C is guilty. However, there is only one guilty suspect, and B and C are in agreement. Therefore, B and C both make true statements. A, whose statement is false, is guilty.

SUMMARY SOLUTION

A did it.

Pool Party Push

CONSIDERATIONS

Consider that only one of the four suspects speaks truthfully.

Assume A's statement is false. If so, neither B nor C is guilty. Therefore, the guilty party is either A or D. Without any more information, however, we cannot determine which one is guilty. Therefore, A's statement is the true one. Either B or C did it. B's statement must be false; C is guilty.

SUMMARY SOLUTION
C did it.

The Impostor Surgeon

CONSIDERATIONS
Consider that the guilty party makes one true and one false statement.

Assume B is the impostor. If so, B's statements are both false. Therefore, B is not the impostor. Assume that C is the impostor. If so, both of C's statements are true. Therefore, C is not the impostor. Therefore, A is the impostor. His first statement is false and second statement is true.

SUMMARY SOLUTION
A did it.

Granny Smith's Famous Pecan Pie

CONSIDERATIONS
Consider that only one suspect speaks the truth.

Assume that A is guilty. If so, his statement and B's are both true. Therefore, A is not guilty. Assume that B is guilty. If so, the statements by B and D are both true. Therefore, B didn't do it. Assume that C is guilty. If so, all four statements are false. Therefore, C is not guilty.

C's statement is the only true one; D is guilty.

SUMMARY SOLUTION
D is guilty.

Two Scam Hustlers

CONSIDERATIONS
Consider that the two guilty parties make false statements; the others make true statements.

Assume that B is guilty. If so, from B's statement, C is also guilty. If so, from C's statement, D is also guilty. Therefore, since there are only two guilty parties, B is not guilty.

Therefore, from B's statement, C is not guilty; from C's statement, D is not guilty; from D's statement, A is guilty; and from A's statement, E is guilty.

SUMMARY SOLUTION
A and E are guilty.

Who Stole the Goat?

CONSIDERATIONS

Consider that the quarterback and the center make two false statements; the running back makes one true and one false statement; and the defensive end makes two true statements.

Suspect D's first statement must be true. D is the running back, as he is the only one who can make that statement. Therefore, his second statement is false; the quarterback did not do it.

A's first statement is true. Therefore, he is the defensive end. The first statements of B and C are false: B is the quarterback and C is the center.

A's second statement is the only other true one; the center did it.

SUMMARY SOLUTION

A is the defensive end.
B is the quarterback.
C is the center.
D is the running back.
The center did it.

What's the Crime?

CONSIDERATIONS

Consider that each suspect makes one true and two false statements.

A's third statement is true, so his other statements are false. Therefore, B is the guilty party.

Since we know that A is innocent, C's third statement is true, so his other statements are false. Therefore, B's first statement is true.

B is guilty of robbing a service station.

SUMMARY SOLUTION

B robbed a service station.

The Hood-Ornament Thefts

CONSIDERATIONS

Consider that only one of the guilty party's statements is true.

Assume that B is guilty. If so, both of B's statements are false. Therefore, B is not the culprit.

Assume that C is guilty. If so, both of C's statements are true. Therefore, C is not guilty.

Assume that D did it. If so, both of D's statements are false. Therefore, D is not guilty.

A did it. His first statement is false and second statement is true.

SUMMARY SOLUTION

A is guilty.

Thanksgiving Dinner

CONSIDERATIONS

Consider that each of the suspects makes at least one false statement.

Assume A is the culprit. If so, A's and B's statements are true. Therefore, A is not guilty.

Assume that B is guilty. If so, again A's and B's statements are true. B did not do it.

C is the guilty party. All statements are false.

SUMMARY SOLUTION

C is the culprit.

Car Thefts

CONSIDERATIONS

Consider that one suspect makes three true statements, and one makes three false statements. How the third suspect responds is unknown.

A's second statement must be false. Otherwise, it would be a contradiction. Therefore, at least one of his statements is true. A is the suspect whose truthfulness is unknown.

B's second statement admits to an untruthful statement. B must be the suspect with three false statements, and C the suspect with all true statements. From B's first statement, which must be false, B is guilty.

SUMMARY SOLUTION
B did it.

Residential Burglaries

CONSIDERATIONS
Consider that each suspect makes at least two false statements.

Assume that A is the burglar, as his second statement claims. If so, his third statement—that B's statement that C is the burglar is false—must be true. Therefore, since A would have at least two true statements, he cannot be guilty.

Assume that C is the burglar. If so, B's second statement is truthful, and B's third statement disputing

A's third statement (that B's second statement is false) is also truthful. Therefore, C is not the burglar.

Therefore, B is the burglar. His first statement, that he doesn't know C, is false, as are his second and third statements. A's first and second statements are false, and C's first and third statements are false. B is guilty.

SUMMARY SOLUTION

B is the burglar.

Who Cheated at Poker?

CONSIDERATIONS

Consider that each player makes one true and one false statement.

First, assume A is guilty. If so, both of A's statements are false. Therefore, A did not do it.

Assume that B is guilty. If so, both of B's statements are true. Therefore, B did not do it.

Now, assume that C is guilty. If so, both of C's statements are false. Therefore, C did not do it.

Assume that D did it. If so, both of D's statements are false. Therefore, D is innocent. Therefore, E did it. E's first statement is true and second statement is false.

SUMMARY SOLUTION
E is guilty.

Which of the Three Is Innocent?

CONSIDERATIONS
Consider that the two culprits truthfully confess their crimes, but the innocent boy falsely confesses to one. Each boy makes one true and two false statements.

Assume that Junior is innocent. If so, Timmy's first statement must be his true statement, and his second and third statements must be false. However, if Junior is innocent, Timmy's third statement is true. Therefore, Junior is not innocent.

Assume that Timmy is innocent. If so, all three of Junior's statements are true. Therefore, Timmy is not innocent.

Therefore, Sonny is innocent.

SUMMARY SOLUTION
Sonny did not do it.

Who Put the Rattlesnake in Henry's Garage?

CONSIDERATIONS

Consider that all statements are true except for any directly mentioning the culprit.

Assume that B is guilty. If so, B's first statement must be true. It claims that A's first statement, that C is not guilty, is false. Since there is only one guilty party, B is innocent.

Assume that C is guilty. If so, B's second statement confirms C's first statement. If C were guilty, B's second statement, which refers directly to C, would deny the truth of C's first statement. Therefore, C is not the guilty party.

Therefore, A is the culprit. B's first statement and C's second statement are both false.

SUMMARY SOLUTION

A did it.

Stolen Golf Clubs

CONSIDERATIONS

Consider that no two suspects make the same number of true statements.

Assume that B is guilty. If so, B's first statement is true, and second and third statements are false. A's first statement is true, and second and third statements are false. C's second statement is true, and first and third statements are false. So B is not guilty.

Assume that C is guilty. If so, C's first and second statements are true and third statement is false. B's first and second statements are true and third statement is false. Therefore, C did not do it. A is guilty. His first statement is true; B's statements are all true; and C's first and second statements are true.

SUMMARY SOLUTION

A is guilty.

Who Stole the Baseball Mitt?

CONSIDERATIONS

Consider that each suspect makes the same number of true and false statements.

Assume that B is the culprit. If so, B has at least two false statements, and C has at least two true ones. Therefore, B is not guilty.

Assume C is guilty. If so, A's first and third statements

are consistent with B's third and first statements. However, their second statements contradict each other; one is true and one is false. Therefore, they have different numbers of true statements. Therefore, C is not guilty.

A did it. Each suspect has one true and two false statements.

SUMMARY SOLUTION
A did it.

Who Stole Golf Cart No. 22?

CONSIDERATIONS
Consider that only one makes no false statements.

A's first and third statements are false, as all four were present. C's first statement agrees with A's first statement, so it too is false. D's first statement contradicts C's third statement, which truthfully claims A's third statement is false.

Therefore, the only reveler with three true statements is B. As indicated by B's second statement, C is guilty.

SUMMARY SOLUTION
C is guilty.

Unsavory Characters

CONSIDERATIONS

Consider that the culprit makes one true and two false statements.

Assume A is guilty. If so, all three of his statements are false. Therefore, A did not do it.

Assume that B is guilty. If so, B's first two statements are true. Therefore, B is innocent.

Assume that C is the guilty party. If so, his first and third statements are true. Therefore, C did not do it.

Therefore, D did it. His first statement is true, and his second and third statements are false.

SUMMARY SOLUTION

D is guilty.

Who Is the Shoplifter?

CONSIDERATIONS

Consider that the culprit makes three false statements; one of the other suspects makes two true and one false statement; and one makes one true and two false statements.

A's first and third statements contradict each other;

one is true and one is false. Therefore, A cannot be the guilty suspect.

Assume that C is the culprit. If so, A must be the suspect with two true and one false statement, and B must be the suspect with one true and two false statements. However, B's third statement would be true; and B's first and second statements contradict C's first and third statements. One of B's two statements must be true and the other, false. Therefore, one of C's two statements must be false and the other must be true. Therefore, C is innocent.

Therefore, B is guilty. A has made one true and two false statements; C has made two true and one false statement; and B's three statements are false.

SUMMARY SOLUTION
B is guilty.

LETTERS FOR DIGITS

Subtraction, Three Digits

CONSIDERATIONS

The digits are 0, 4, and 8.

```
    (3) (2) (1)
     A   C   A
   - C   C   C
   ―――――――――――
     C   B   C
```

From column 2, B must be 0. This leaves 4 and 8 available. Therefore, from columns 1 and 3, A must be 8 and C must be 4.

SUMMARY SOLUTION

A = 8, B = 0, C = 4

```
    8   4   8
  - 4   4   4
  ───────────
    4   0   4
```

Addition, Four Digits

CONSIDERATIONS

The digits are 1, 2, 3, and 4.

```
   (2) (1)
    A   A
  + B   C
  ───────
    C   D
```

Given the available digits, since A plus B equals C in column 2, C must be 3. C could not be 4, as, from column 1, D would have to be larger than 4 (no larger digit is available). Therefore, A is 1, D is 4, and B is 2.

SUMMARY SOLUTION

A = 1, B = 2, C = 3, D = 4

$$
\begin{array}{cc}
\mathbf{1} & \mathbf{1} \\
+\ \mathbf{2} & \mathbf{3} \\
\hline
\mathbf{3} & \mathbf{4}
\end{array}
$$

Subtraction, Four Digits

CONSIDERATIONS

The digits are 2, 4, 6, and 8.

$$
\begin{array}{ccc}
\mathbf{(3)} & \mathbf{(2)} & \mathbf{(1)} \\
\mathbf{A} & \mathbf{B} & \mathbf{C} \\
-\ \mathbf{B} & \mathbf{D} & \mathbf{D} \\
\hline
\mathbf{D} & \mathbf{D} & \mathbf{B}
\end{array}
$$

From columns 2 and 3, B minus D equals D, and A minus B equals D. Considering the available digits, the only possibility for D is 2. If D were 4, B would be 8, and this won't work for B in column 3 or column 1. Therefore, B equals 4 and A must be 6. C is the remaining digit, 8.

SUMMARY SOLUTION
A = 6, B = 4, C = 8, D = 2

$$
\begin{array}{r}
6\ \ 4\ \ 8 \\
-\ 4\ \ 2\ \ 4 \\
\hline
2\ \ 2\ \ 4
\end{array}
$$

Addition, Five Digits

CONSIDERATIONS
The digits are 1, 2, 3, 4, and 5.

$$
\begin{array}{r}
(3)\ (2)\ (1) \\
A\ \ A\ \ E \\
+\ E\ \ A\ \ C \\
\hline
B\ \ D\ \ D
\end{array}
$$

From columns 1 and 2, given the available digits, the only possibility for D is 4. Therefore, from column 2, A equals 2. From column 3, B must be 5, and E equals 3. Therefore, C is 1.

SUMMARY SOLUTION
A = 2, B = 5 C = 1 D = 4

$$
\begin{array}{r}
2\ \ 2\ \ 3 \\
+\ 3\ \ 2\ \ 1 \\
\hline
5\ \ 4\ \ 4
\end{array}
$$

Addition, Six Digits

CONSIDERATIONS

The digits are 0, 2, 3, 4, 5, and 6.

```
  (5) (4) (3) (2) (1)
   A   E   A   C   A
 + E   E   A   B   D
 ─────────────────────
   F   C   D   C   C
```

From column 2, B is 0, since C plus B equals C. From columns 3 and 4, A plus A equals 4 or 6, and E equals 2 or 3. E plus E must equal 4 or 6. Therefore, F, column 5, must equal 5. From column 1, A plus D equals C. Therefore, A must equal 2, D equals 4, and C equals 6.

SUMMARY SOLUTION

A = 2, B = 0, C = 6, D = 4, E = 3, F = 5

```
     2   3   2   6   2
 +   3   3   2   0   4
 ─────────────────────
     5   6   4   6   6
```

Addition, Six Digits Again

CONSIDERATIONS

The digits are 0, 1, 3, 5, 7, and 9.

```
(5)(4)(3)(2)(1)
    B  C  E  C
+   E  C  E  F
─────────────
 A  E  E  A  D
```

From column 5, A must be a carry of 1 from column 4. Therefore, from column 2, E must be 5: 5 + 5 + a carry of 1 from column 1. From column 3, C must be 7 considering a carry of 1 from column 2. From column 4, B + 5 + a carry of 1 from column 3 is 15. Therefore, B is 9. From column 1, F is 3 and D is 0.

SUMMARY SOLUTION

A = 1, B = 9, C = 7, D = 0, E = 5, F = 3

```
    9  7  5  7
+   5  7  5  3
─────────────
 1  5  5  1  0
```

Subtraction, Five Digits

CONSIDERATIONS

The digits are 2, 3, 5, 7, and 9.

(3)	(2)	(1)
A	C	E
− C	E	D
F	F	F

From columns 1, 2, and 3, considering the available digits, 2 is the only digit that could represent F in all three columns. From column 1, E minus D must be 9 minus 7, 7 minus 5, or 5 minus 3.

From column 2, C minus E equals 2. Therefore, E cannot be 9. If E is 7, C must be 9. However, from column 3, C cannot be 9. Therefore, from column 1, E is 5 and D is 3. From column 2, C is 7. The remaining letter, A, is 9.

SUMMARY SOLUTION

A = 9,   C = 7,   D = 3,   E = 5,   F = 2

9	7	5
− 7	5	3
2	2	2

Addition, Eight Digits

CONSIDERATIONS

The digits are 0, 1, 2, 3, 4, 5, 6, and 7.

```
  (5) (4) (3) (2) (1)
   C   D   A   F   C
+  C   D   C   B   H
―――――――――――――――――――――
H  E   C   E   G   F
```

C, column 5, must be 5, 6, or 7, since there is a carry in the answer to C plus C, and H, which represents the carry, must be 1. Since we know that H equals 1, F, the sum of C plus H in column 1, must equal one more than C. Therefore, F must equal 6 or 7 and C must equal 5 or 6. A, column 3, must be 1 less than C, since the sum of A plus C plus a possible carry equals C plus C plus a possible carry, column 5. D, column 4, must be 2 or 3, since the sum of D plus D, plus possibly a carry from column 3 equals C.

If C is 6, A is 5, F is 7, and D is 3. However, from column 3, A plus C would require a carry to column 4, which would make C 7. Therefore, C must be 5, A is 4, and F is 6. Therefore, E is 0: the sum of C plus C, column 5. D is 2. The two remaining letters, B and G, are 7 and 3, respectively, since, from column 2, F 6 plus B 7 equals G 3 plus a carry to column 4.

SUMMARY SOLUTION

A = 4,   B = 7,   C = 5,   D = 2,   E = 0,   F = 6,   G = 3,   H = 1

```
      5   2   4   6   5
  +   5   2   5   7   1
  ─────────────────────
  1   0   5   0   3   6
```

Addition, Eight Digits Again

CONSIDERATIONS

The digits are 2, 3, 4, 5, 6, 7, 8, and 9.

```
 (5) (4)(3)(2)(1)
              B   C
      E   E   F   E   C
      E   H   D   H   A
  +   H   E   A   E   H
  ─────────────────────
      F   G   G   B   H
```

From columns 5 and 4, F is 7 or 8, E is 2 or 3, and H is 2 or 3. No other possibilities exist without a carry to a sixth column.

From column 4, G is 8 or 9. Therefore, from column 1, given the available digits, C plus C plus A must equal 20. Therefore, there is a carry of 2 to column 2, making the total of 10 for the two E's and one H plus the carry of 2 from column 1. Therefore, from columns 5 and 4, E is 3, H is 2, F is 8, and G is 9. From column 3, D plus A equals ten plus a carry of one from column 2. Therefore, D is 6 or 4, and A is 6 or 4. From column 1, C must be 7, and A is 6. Therefore, D is 4. By elimination, B is 5.

SUMMARY SOLUTION

A = 6, B = 5, C = 7, D = 4, E = 3, F = 8, G = 9 H = 2

$$
\begin{array}{rrrrr}
 & & & 5 & 7 \\
3 & 3 & 8 & 3 & 7 \\
3 & 2 & 4 & 2 & 6 \\
+\,2 & 3 & 6 & 3 & 2 \\
\hline
8 & 9 & 9 & 5 & 2 \\
\end{array}
$$

Addition, Seven Digits

CONSIDERATIONS

The digits are 1, 2, 3, 4, 5, 7, and 8.

```
(7) (6) (5) (4) (3) (2) (1)
    G   D   B   E   G   A
    D   D   F   B   A   A
+   D   G   C   B   A   A
─────────────────────────────
A   E   G   A   B   C   G
```

Column 7 represents a carry from column 6. A must be 1 or 2. From column 1, A is 1 and G is 3, since no digit is available for G if A were 2.

From columns 5 and 6, since the sums of D, D, and G are different for the two columns, column 5 includes a carry of two from column 4, and column 6 represents a carry of one from column 4. B plus F plus a carry must equal 16. Therefore, B is 7 or 8.

From column 3, B must be 8, as 7 will not work. Therefore, E is 2 and F is 7. From column 2, C is 5. From column 2, F is 7, and from column 5, D is 4.

SUMMARY SOLUTION

A = 1, B = 8, C = 5, D = 4, E = 2, F = 6, G = 3

```
    3  4  8  2  3  1
    4  4  7  8  1  1
 +  4  3  5  8  1  1
 ─────────────────────
 1  2  3  1  8  5  3
```

DESERT FOOTHILLS GOLF

The First Decision

CONSIDERATIONS

Consider that at least one of the signs is false.

Assume that path A is the path to take. If so, sign A is true. However, since at least one of the signs is false, sign B would have to be false. There is no way to validate sign B as being false. Therefore, sign A is false, as is sign B. Path B is the path to take.

	sign A	sign B
If path A	T	T
If path B	F	F

SUMMARY SOLUTION

Path B is correct.

The Second Decision

CONSIDERATIONS

Consider that the correct decision can conclusively be made.

Assume that path B is the correct path. If so, sign B is true and sign C is false. However, it is impossible to decide conclusively whether sign A is true or false. If it is true, it is false; if it is false, it is true. The same conclusion must be drawn if the assumption is made that path C is the one to take. Therefore, path A is the one to take.

	sign A	sign B	sign C
If path A	T	F	F
If path B	T/F	T	F
If path C	T/F	F	T

SUMMARY SOLUTION

Path A is the correct path.

The Third Decision

CONSIDERATIONS

Consider that only one of the signs is true.

Assume that path A is the correct choice. If so, the sign at path A is true, the sign at path B is false, and the sign at path C is true. Therefore, path A is not the right choice. Assume that path B is the right one. If so, the sign at path A is false, and the signs at paths B and C are both true. Therefore, path C is correct: the sign at path A is true and the signs at paths B and C are both false.

	sign A	sign B	sign C
If path A	T	F	T
If path B	F	T	T
If path C	T	F	F

SUMMARY SOLUTION
Take path C.

The Fourth Decision

CONSIDERATIONS
Consider that at least one sign is false.

Assume that path B is correct. If so, all three signs are true. Assume that path C is the right path. Again, if so, all three signs are true. Therefore, path A is the correct path. All three signs are false.

	sign A	sign B	sign C
If path A	F	F	F
If path B	T	T	T
If path C	T	T	T

SUMMARY SOLUTION
Path A is the right path.

The Fifth Decision

CONSIDERATIONS
Consider that exactly one of the signs is false.

Assume that path A is the correct path. If so, the sign at path A is false, as is the sign at path B. (The sign at path C can be true or false, but that's immaterial, since there are already two false signs.) Therefore, path A is not the way to go. Assume that path C is right. If so, the sign at path A is true.

However, the signs at paths B and C are both false. Therefore, path B is the correct path: the sign at path A is false and the signs at paths B and C must both be true.

If path A	F	F	T/F
If path B	F	T	T
If path C	T	F	F

SUMMARY SOLUTION

Path B is the one to take.

The Sixth Decision

CONSIDERATION

Consider that exactly one sign is false.

Assume that path A is correct. If so, the sign at path A is true; however, the signs at paths B and C are both false. Therefore, path A is not the way to go. Assume that path C is correct. If so, the sign at path A is true, and the signs at paths B and C are both false. Therefore, the path to take is B.

	sign A	sign B	sign C
If path A	T	F	F
If path B	F	T	T
If path C	T	F	F

SUMMARY SOLUTION

Path B is the correct path.

The Seventh Decision

CONSIDERATIONS

Consider that the sign at the path to take is the only false one.

If path B is the correct path, the sign at path B is false. But then the sign at path C cannot be true, since only one sign is false. So path B is not correct.

If path C is the correct path, the sign at path C is false and the sign at path A must be true. But this is impossible. So path C is not the correct path. The correct path is path A. The sign at path A is false, the sign at path B is true, and the sign at path C is true.

	sign A	sign B	sign C
If path A	F	T	T
If path B	T	F	F
If path C	F	T	F

SUMMARY SOLUTION

Take path A.

The Eighth Decision

CONSIDERATIONS

Consider that one or more signs are false.

Assume that path A is correct. If so, the sign at path A is true, as are the signs at B and C. Assume that path C is the right path. If so, all three signs are true. Therefore, B is the correct path: the sign at path A is true, the sign at path B is false, and the sign at path C is true.

	sign A	sign B	sign C
If path A	T	T	T
If path B	T	F	T
If path C	T	T	T

SUMMARY SOLUTION
Path B is the correct path.

The Ninth Decision

CONSIDERATIONS
Consider that at least two signs are false.

Assume that path A will lead to the clubhouse. If so, all three signs are true. Therefore, path A is not the way to go. Assume that path B is correct. If so, the sign at path A is false, and the sign at path B is true, as is the sign at path C. Therefore, path C is the way to the clubhouse. All three signs are false.

	sign A	sign B	sign C
If path A	T	T	T
If path B	F	T	T
If path C	F	F	F

SUMMARY SOLUTION
Path C will lead to the clubhouse.

NAMESAKES

Four Fishing Boats

CONSIDERATIONS

From statement 2, Jeb's horse is named King. Therefore, King is not the name of his fishing boat.

From statements 3 and 4, Jeb's fishing boat is not named Ace or Beau. Therefore, Jeb's fishing boat is named Spike. Since Joe's fishing boat is named Ace (statement 3), Jake's fishing boat must be named King or Beau.

From statement 1, Jake's fishing boat is named after Jay's horse. Therefore, since Jeb's horse is named King, Jay's horse and Jake's fishing boat are both named Beau.

Therefore, Jay's fishing boat is named King. Since Joe's fishing boat is named Ace, his horse must be named Spike, and Jake's horse is named Ace.

SUMMARY SOLUTION

	Horse	**Boat**
Jake	Ace	Beau
Jay	Beau	King
Jeb	King	Spike
Joe	Spike	Ace

Knowheyan Paddle-Bird Tournament

CONSIDERATIONS

From statement 1, the visitor Larry was not teamed with the inhabitant Lenny. Therefore, the visitor Larry was teamed with either the Knowheyan Logan or Lewis.

From statement 2, the visitor Lenny was not teamed with the Knowheyan Larry. Therefore, the visitor Lenny was teamed with the Knowheyan Logan or Lewis.

From statement 3, the visitor Logan was not teamed with the Knowheyan Lewis. Therefore, the visitor Logan was teamed with either the Knowheyan Larry or Lenny.

From statement 4, the visitor Logan was teamed with the Knowheyan Larry. Therefore, the visitor Larry was teamed with the Knowheyan Lewis, the visitor Lenny was teamed with the Knowheyan Logan, and, by elimination, the visitor Lewis was teamed with the Knowheyan Lenny.

SUMMARY SOLUTION

Visitor Larry — Knowheyan Lewis
Visitor Lenny — Knowheyan Logan
Visitor Logan — Knowheyan Larry
Visitor Lewis — Knowheyan Lenny

Burglaries in the Neighborhood

CONSIDERATIONS

From statements 1, 3, and 6, Milton's dog is not named Moriarity, Maurice, Martin, or Marion; therefore, Milton's dog is Melville. Therefore, from statement 5, Martin's dog is named Milton, and, from statement 1, Melville's dog is named Moriarity. From statement 2, Moriarity owns the dog named Marion.

Therefore, Maurice's dog is named Martin, and Marion's dog is named Maurice. From statement 4, the burglar is Moriarity.

SUMMARY SOLUTION

Marion's dog is Maurice

Martin's dog is Milton

Maurice's dog is Martin

Melville's dog is Moriarity

Milton's dog is Melville

Moriarity's dog is Marion

The burglar is Moriarity.

THINGS IN ORDER
Wood-Chopping Contest

SOLUTION

1. Egum	7. Estum
2. Epum	8. Esum
3. Elfum	9. Edum
4. Efrum	10. Ebum
5. Ekum	11. Eskum
6. Evum	12. Ensum

Trees in the Forest

SOLUTION

One side of the path	Other side of the path
9. maple	hickory
8. oak	poplar
7. elm	ash
6. willow	tamarack
5. fir	yew
4. cedar	spruce
3. birch	juniper
2. hemlock	alder
1. pine	aspen

Fishing Flies

SOLUTION

1. Murphy's No. 1	9. Royal Humpy
2. Adams	10. Wright's Royal
3. Olive Blue Dun	11. Elk-Hair Caddis
4. Gold-Ribbed Hare's Ear	12. Light Cahill
5. Woolly Bugger	13. Prince Nymph
6. Maribou Muddler	14. Brook's Stone Fly
7. Royal Wulff	15. Zug Bug
8. Grey Wulff	16. Joe's Hopper

Varieties of Fruit

SOLUTION

Back row: pears, oranges, peaches, plums, cherries, loquats, persimmons, apricots, papayas, guavas.

Front row: limes, watermelons, bananas, blackberries, strawberries, raspberries, lemons, mangos, nectarines, grapes.

New Neighbors

SOLUTION

Left to right facing east	Right to left facing west
1. Maloneys	Mahoneys
2. Mayers	Marshalls
3. Maxwells	Mathesons
4. Mallettes	Marleaus
5. Marlows	Martins
6. Mayburys	Majors
7. Malones	Magnans
8. Mastersons	Marquardts
9. Mallorys	Marsdens
10. Marshes	Mathews
11. Mayfields	Matsens
12. Matlocks	Macklins

INDEX

Illustration Credits

Illustrations appearing in this book between pages 8 and 25 by Elise Chanowitz

Illustrations appearing in this book between pages 26 and 65 by Jack Williams

Illustrations appearing in this book between pages 66 and 91 by Jim Sharpe

Illustrations appearing in this book between pages 160 and 268 provided by Norman D. Willis

WHAT IS MENSA?

Mensa—The High IQ Society

Mensa is the international society for people with a high IQ. We have more than 100,000 members in over 40 countries worldwide.

The society's aims are:

- To identify and foster human intelligence for the benefit of humanity;
- To encourage research in the nature, characteristics, and uses of intelligence;
- To provide a stimulating intellectual and social environment for its members.

Anyone with an IQ score in the top two percent of the population is eligible to become a member of Mensa—are you the "one in 50" we've been looking for?

Mensa membership offers an excellent range of benefits:

- Networking and social activities nationally and around the world;
- Special Interest Groups (hundreds of chances to pursue your hobbies and interests—from art to zoology!);
- Monthly International Journal, national magazines, and regional newsletters;
- Local meetings—from game challenges to food and drink;
- National and international weekend gatherings and conferences;
- Intellectually stimulating lectures and seminars;
- Access to the worldwide SIGHT network for travelers and hosts.

**For more information about
Mensa International:**

www.mensa.org
Mensa International
15 The Ivories
6–8 Northampton Street
Islington, London N1 2HY
United Kingdom

**For more information about
American Mensa:**

www.us.mensa.org
Telephone: (800) 66-MENSA
American Mensa Ltd.
1229 Corporate Drive West
Arlington, TX 76006-6103 US

**For more information about
British Mensa (UK and Ireland):**

www.mensa.org.uk
Telephone: +44 (0) 1902 772771
E-mail: enquiries@mensa.org.uk
British Mensa Ltd.
St. John's House
St. John's Square
Wolverhampton WV2 4AH
United Kingdom